New Searchlight Series

Under the general editorship of
George W. Hoffman and G. Etzel Pearcy

S0-BJR-836

HaFt
C1
1A
Geog436
·Aice

The South

Second Edition

John Fraser Hart

University of Minnesota

 D. VAN NOSTRAND COMPANY

New York · Cincinnati · Toronto · London · Melbourne

D. Van Nostrand Company Regional Offices:
New York   Cincinnati   Millbrae

D. Van Nostrand Company International Offices:
London   Toronto   Melbourne

Library of Congress Catalog Card Number: 75–16550
ISBN: 0–442–29754–8

Published by D. Van Nostrand Company
450 West 33rd Street, New York, N.Y.   10001

10   9   8   7   6   5   4   3   2   1

Preface

The purpose of this book is to introduce the reader to the Southern United States and to help him understand this vital section of our nation. The reader who wishes to understand this region must realize that there is not one South, but many, and thus the theme of regional diversity within the South is one of the two principal motifs which runs through this book. The other is the theme of paradox, for each part of the South has many faces, and these faces are often cheek by jowl.

The startling contrasts characteristic of the South will be noticed by an observant traveler passing through many a small town in the region. On one side of the street, or at one corner of the block, is the New South—new buildings, neat, prosperous-looking, all glass, chrome, and glazed yellow brick. The New South is modern, up-to-date, spic and span, progressive.

But across the street, or at the other end of the block, or around the corner, is the Old South. The buildings are of tired red brick, with weatherbeaten wooden benches on the trash-littered street in front of them. An arcade of rusty metal roofing, which sticks out over the benches to ward off summer sun and winter rains, adds to the general impression of somnolence and decay. The Old South is backward, decrepit, forlorn, depressing.

Time after time, in place after place, the New South and the

Old South are quietly side by side. He who seeks bad in the South can find it in abundance, but so also can he who seeks good; the greatest difficulties confront him who seeks to achieve and maintain a balanced view of the region.

The paradoxical character of the South is reflected in the revised edition of this book. The region has experienced enormous changes since the first edition appeared, yet many of the basic ingredients of its geography have remained virtually unchanged. The statistical material has been updated, and some sections—especially those dealing with cities, industry, and politics—have been completely rewritten to reflect the changes which have occurred, but large segments of the original work have required little or no modification.

As a child (and later, student) of the South, I can appreciate all too well the audacity of trying to describe and explain, much less understand, this fascinating land of paradox. Much of what I know about this complex region I have learned from others. I should like to express my sincere appreciation to Meredith D. Hart, Richard Hartshorne, Eugene Cotton Mather, Merle Prunty, Wilbur Zelinsky, and the members of my family, each of whom has taught me much about the South and its people.

JOHN FRASER HART

Contents

	Preface	iii
1	The South: An Overview	1
2	Cotton Belt No Longer	25
3	New Uses for Old Lands	43
4	Tobacco Country	70
5	The Border Hills	78
6	The Limestone Lowlands	99
7	The Growth Coast	108
8	The New South	130
	Suggestions for Further Reading	155
	Selected Topographic Maps	158
	Index	161

Maps

1	Percentage of Families Below Low Income Level in 1970	8
2	Population Change between 1940 and 1970	12
3	Major Cities	15
4	Agricultural Specialty Areas	26
5	Landforms (after Hammond)	44
6	Land Types (after Barnes and Marschner)	45
7	Woodland	46
8	Forest Fires	51
9	Pulpwood Mills	53
10	Forest Industry Land	55
11	Index of Mining Employment	87

12   Cropland   100
13   Pasture and Grazing Land   101
14   Military Personnel   136
15   Population Density   140
16   Index of Manufacturing Employment   142
17   Types of Counties   145
18   Eisenhower-Nixon Vote   151
19   Nixon-Agnew Vote in 1972   153

Tables

1   Median family income, 1969   6
2   The South's share of the national total, 1960
    and 1970   7
3   Population of twenty largest urbanized areas   14
4   Cotton in six Southern states, 1900–1970   34

1 The South: An Overview

If the South has a symbol, it is the statue of the Confederate soldier which stands in the county seat. Hands resting on the barrel of his grounded rifle, knapsack and blanket roll on his back, he stares in stony silence to the north whence came the invading Yankee armies. For almost a century he has served as a reminder of the drastic changes wrought by the Civil War, which burned a traumatic scar across the mind of the South. Before the war the South was one of the dominant sections of the United States; afterward it languished into a stagnant backwater outside the mainstream of American national life.

The South had been one of the first parts of the United States to be settled and developed. Virginians like to remember that prosperous Tidewater tobacco farmers had already imported a boatload of Negro slaves to work their fields before the *Mayflower* first set sail from Plymouth. Mississippians boast that a third of all the millionaires in the United States just before the Civil War lived in Natchez.

The voices of Southern orators had reverberated along the national corridors of power. Four of the first five presidents of the nation were Virginians, and nine of the first twelve were natives of the South. Southerners virtually guaranteed the election of Abraham Lincoln as the sixteenth president when they withdrew from the national Democratic party and nominated John C. Breckinridge as their own candidate in opposition to Stephen A. Douglas, the candidate of the national party.

Then came the Civil War, which shattered the political power of the South and desolated its economy. At the end of the war one out of every four able-bodied Southern men of military age had been killed in battle, had died of wounds, or had returned home maimed. The capital invested in the newly emancipated slaves (perhaps a billion dollars or more) had been wiped out, without the recompense to their former owners that President Abraham Lincoln had recommended, and the currency was worthless.

Richmond, Columbia, Atlanta, Jackson, and many other Southern cities had been gutted by fire, pillagers had taken millions of dollars worth of goods from their rightful owners, and business was paralyzed. The Federal government had confiscated cotton that had been stored in warehouses for lack of an export market during the war. Canal and harbor works had been wrecked, and practically all railroads and bridges had been demolished. Hundreds of public buildings and thousands of private homes had been destroyed. The shame and humiliation of having lost the war were compounded when proud Southerners were subjected to military occupation by a conquering army, an ignominy which the people of no other section of the nation have been forced to endure.

"THE NATION'S NUMBER ONE ECONOMIC PROBLEM"

For three generations, while the rest of the nation rolled up its sleeves and went to work, Southerners looked backward and dreamed of a past which had never existed. While the rest of the United States was rushing pell-mell to industrialize, the South persisted in a semicolonial economy, exporting staple crops and raw materials, and importing most of the manufactured goods it needed.

Although the region remained predominantly agricultural, its agriculture presented the paradox of poverty amidst potential plenty. Southerners are still trying to work out a system of production which can develop the region's natural resources for effective production and equitable distribution of its riches. For three-quarters of a century after the Civil War the South remained a one-crop area, because its landlords and tenants could not agree on a workable method for financing, producing, and sharing the profits from crops other than cotton and tobacco. As late as 1938 the farming South depended upon cotton and tobacco for two-thirds of its cash income, and more than half of its farmers depended upon cotton alone.

Farm income was so pitifully low that the region produced no surplus which could be invested in industry or in the infrastructure necessary for economic development. Vast power resources remained untapped, transportation facilities were inadequate, and education and housing conditions were a national disgrace. The industrial development which occurred in scattered locations was also semicolonial; based largely on the processing of local raw materials such as cotton and tobacco, it was financed and controlled by outside capital, and its profits were siphoned out of the region.

Three-quarters of a century after the end of the Civil War, President Roosevelt could point to the South as "the nation's number one economic problem." As in many underdeveloped areas of the contemporary world, outside assistance was crucially important for any economic development in the South. In a sense, this region was the laboratory in which the United States first experimented with techniques of assisting underdeveloped areas, techniques which have been applied in so many different parts of the world since the end of the Second World War.

Federal agencies helped farmers by providing inexpensive credit and improved marketing facilities, by suggesting soil conservation practices and changes in land tenure, and by assisting with road construction and rural electrification. Water development and conservation programs, such as those of the TVA, helped the South by generating more power, controlling floods, and improving river navigation. The Defense Plant Corporation and other wartime agencies channelled industry into the South during the Second World War.

Since 1945 many Southerners have worked actively to develop the great potential of their region. Many members of the fourth generation have begun to forget the Civil War, and to recognize the fact that they are Americans first, and Southerners second. Most Southern states have waged aggressive campaigns to attract new industry by emphasizing their advantages of cheap labor, abundant power and raw materials, and a rapidly growing regional market, but they have done so in an era when manufacturing activities have ceased to be the magic touchstone to healthy economic growth.

Despite the startling transformations which have been made in some areas, the South still has many pockets of bitter poverty and underdevelopment. Although Southerners are quite properly proud of the progress they have made in recent years, the rest of the nation is impatient for the South to make even more rapid progress in solving some of the problems which still remain. The fiercest passions have been aroused by the reluctance of white Southerners to accord black people their full rights as members of the human race, but race relations is only one of the problems that beset the contemporary South. Far too many Southerners are still far too eager to point to the racial problems of cities outside the South, and too reluctant to admit that they have problems right in their own back yards.

Although the South has finally started to catch up with the rest of the nation, it still has quite a long way to go. When Southerners boast of their region's progress, they are fond of quoting percentage increases, but cynical observers note that the South has been so far behind the rest of the nation that a large percentage increase sometimes masks a rather slight actual increase. For example, in 1939 the four West South Central states (Arkansas, Louisiana, Oklahoma, and Texas) had 331,000 workers employed in manufacturing, whereas Greater New York alone had 1,117,000. By 1959 the number of manufacturing workers in these four states had increased 133 percent, as against only 48 percent in Greater New York. Such statistics are quite impressive until you realize that the total increase of 441,000 new workers in the West South Central states was 103,000 workers less than the total increase of 544,000 new workers in Greater New York alone. It reminds one of the story of the village in Siberia where the Communist party chief reported a wedding by announcing that two percent of the men had married fifty percent of the women.

POOR QUARTER OF THE NATION

How *does* the South actually stack up against the rest of the nation? To begin with, it is a large area. The 1,600 miles which separate Baltimore from San Antonio are only slightly less than the distance from New York City to eastern Colorado, or Kansas City to San Francisco, or New Orleans to Winnipeg, or London to Moscow. The sixteen states of the South cover approximately 900,000 square miles, an area approximately the size of Western Europe. This is almost one-quarter of the total area of the United States, and it is the poorest quarter.

No matter what criterion of poverty is used, most of the Southern states rank low on the list. In 1969, for example, half of all families in the United States had an income of $9,586 or more, but the median family income in the South was only $8,075, and the median family income in Mississippi was more than $2,000 below even that low figure (see Table 1). Were it not for South Dakota ("the Mississippi of the North") which ranked forty-fourth, the sixteen states of the South would have included the ten poorest states in the Union; they did include thirteen of the eighteen lowest in income.

The United States has a "Poverty Oval" which is focused on the South. Poverty cannot be measured in income terms alone; for example, a single person on a farm ordinarily is able to get by on less money than a large family would need to survive in a city. In 1969 a Federal Interagency Committee adopted a sliding scale of low-income (poverty) level values which varied with size of family, sex and age of the family head, and farm-nonfarm residence; the cutoff values are updated each year to reflect changes in the Consumer Price Index. Nearly half the families in the United States which were below the low-income level in 1970 were in the South; one of every

TABLE 1.   Median family income, 1969

	Total	Rank	White	Negro
UNITED STATES	$9,586		$9,957	$6,063
The South	8,075		8,718	4,897
Mississippi	6,068	50	7,577	3,200
Arkansas	6,271	49	6,827	3,453
Alabama	7,263	48	8,205	4,047
West Virginia	7,414	47	7,493	4,851
Kentucky	7,439	46	7,602	5,128
Tennessee	7,446	45	7,872	4,838
South Dakota	*7,490*	*44*	*7,619*	*5,721*
Louisiana	7,527	43	8,817	4,002
South Carolina	7,620	42	8,760	4,443
Oklahoma	7,720	41	7,997	4,529
North Carolina	7,770	40	8,504	4,798
Georgia	8,165	37	9,176	4,742
Florida	8,261	35	8,812	4,981
Texas	8,486	33	8,926	5,330
Virginia	9,044	25	9,762	5,740
Delaware	10,209	14	10,732	6,399
Maryland	11,057	5	11,629	7,696

six families in the South was living in poverty, as against one in ten for the nation as a whole (Table 2).

The South has two hundred counties in which at least one family in three lives below the poverty level (Fig. 1). The deepest pocket of poverty is in the hills of eastern Kentucky, but the great poverty belt which arcs from Arkansas and Louisiana across Mississippi and Alabama into Georgia is also the area which has the highest percentage of Negroes. In most of the South the median income of Negro families ran around $4,000 a year lower than the median income of white families in 1969 (Table 1).

The miseries of the poverty belt are aggravated by a taxation system which weighs more heavily on poor people than on those with substantial incomes and properties. In February 1974, the Southern Regional Council issued a report which stated that "the lowest income states make the greatest use of those taxes which weigh most heavily on the poor. . . . Compared to all the state averages, the tax effort on regressive sales taxes in the Southern states is high, on progressive income taxes is somewhat lower, and on property taxes it is considerably lower."

TABLE 2. The South's share of the national total, 1960 and 1970

Percentage of the nation's	1960	1970
Total land area	24.7	24.7
Total population	30.6	30.9
Personal income	24.2	26.4
Families below low-income level	48.3	47.0
Housing units with all plumbing facilities	24.6	29.2
Housing units with air conditioning	42.7	43.0
People 25 or older with high school diplomas	25.0	26.2
People 25 or older with less than 5 years school	48.7	49.0
Farm population	44.0	35.9
Farms with sales of less than $10,000	49.6	51.5
Farms with sales of $10,000 or more	24.8	25.8
Commercial forest land	39.4	38.6
Urban population	25.6	27.2
Population in places of 10,000 or more	24.1	26.6
Population in places of 2,500 to 10,000	32.0	33.2
Employed civilian labor force	28.8	29.6
Workers employed in manufacturing	22.6	26.6
Workers employed in services	35.6	34.4
White collar workers	26.3	28.0
Value of mineral production	52.1	56.8
Negro population	60.0	53.0
Population of foreign stock	9.6	12.3

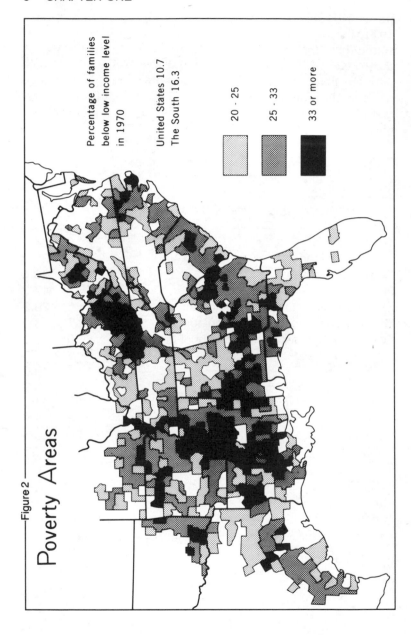

Figure 2
Poverty Areas

Percentage of families
below low income level
in 1970

United States 10.7
The South 16.3

20 - 25

25 - 33

33 or more

STARVATION

On June 16, 1967, a team of four doctors who had made a cursory survey of six poverty belt counties in Mississippi told the Senate Subcommittee on Manpower, Employment and Poverty that "we do not want to quibble over words, but 'malnutrition' is not quite what we found; the boys and girls we saw were . . . suffering from hunger and disease, and directly or indirectly they are dying from them—which is exactly what 'starvation' means."

The poor people of the South have not been able to afford good food or decent housing (Table 2). In the United States as a whole only one house in every twenty lacked adequate plumbing in 1970, but in the South the figure was closer to one in ten, and in Mississippi it was more than one in every five. The South had the seven states with the lowest percentage of inside plumbing and would have had the eleven lowest but for Alaska; at least the poorest quarter of the nation can boast that it is richest in privies. Paradoxically, it is also richest in the number of housing units which have air conditioning, necessitated by the blistering summer weather.

Low levels of income are also reflected in low levels of education, whether measured by school expenditure per capita or per pupil, by teachers' salaries, or by years of school completed by those aged twenty-five and over. More than half of the adult population of the United States in 1970 had graduated from high school, but in large parts of the South three of every five adults still had not received their diplomas (Table 2).

POOR FARM LAND

Much of the poverty of the South can be attributed to the traditional dependence of the region upon agriculture. Most of the South does not have good farm land, farms are too small, and farm production and management practices are backward. For example, the Spring 1974 issue of *Texas Agricultural Progress* concluded an article on dairy farming in East

Texas with the statement that "the application of advanced technology and management could increase production per cow from 9,242 pounds to 14,500 pounds annually, and increase the profit from $1.02 to $2.08 per hundred pounds of milk." This situation in East Texas is not unique in the South.

Between 1960 and 1970 the farm population declined much more rapidly in the South than in the nation as a whole; yet the South still had far more than its share of undersized farms, which produced less than $10,000 worth of farm products each year, and a bit less than its share of farms which produced enough to give the farmer an adequate return for his labor and investment (Table 2).

Recent efforts at diversifying agriculture in the South have slowly borne fruit, but the old standbys are still important. Cotton, once king in most of the region, has been dethroned to the status of just another crop, although still a major crop (Fig. 4). In 1959 cotton was the leading crop in a belt of states across the Plainsland South—first in Texas, Arkansas, Louisiana, Mississippi, Alabama, and Tennessee, and second in Georgia and South Carolina. By 1969 cotton had been replaced by soybeans, the new glamor crop, in much of the South, although it remained first in Texas, Mississippi, and Alabama. Tobacco, the other old reliable, retained its traditional dominance in Kentucky and in the Carolinas, and it remained a major crop in the other states of the eastern seaboard.[1]

The traditional crops of the South have required large forces of labor but relatively little land. A remarkably small proportion of the South is used for cropland (Fig. 12). Even back in the days when cotton was king, for instance, the crop was rarely planted on more than about a tenth of the land of any given county. The principal concentrations of cropland in 1964 were on the Blackland Prairie of Texas, the alluvial lowlands along the Mississippi River, the limestone lowlands of

1. John Fraser Hart and Eugene Cotton Mather, "The Character of Tobacco Barns and Their Role in the Tobacco Economy of the United States," *Annals of the Association of American Geographers*, Vol. 51 (1961), pp. 274–93.

Kentucky and Tennessee, the Coastal Plain of the Carolinas and Georgia, and the Coastal Prairies of Louisiana and Texas. Grazing and pasture land is even less important than cropland (Fig. 13). In the South as a whole about one acre in every five is used for cropland, but only one in ten is used for pasture. The principal concentrations of pasture land are in southern Florida and eastern Texas, especially the Coastal Prairies.

The total amount of farm land in the South, after increasing from about 350 million acres in 1910 to over 390 million acres in 1950, had dropped back to only 330 million acres by 1970.[2] Much of the abandoned farm land quickly reverts to woodland. The amount of woodland is one of the most distinctive features of the rural South (Fig. 7). More than three-fifths of the region is wooded, and nearly two-fifths of the nation's commercial forest land is in the South (Table 2).

PEOPLE LEAVING

Perhaps the most effective solution to many of the agricultural problems of the South would be to get the people off the land, and that is precisely what has been happening at an astonishingly rapid rate. During the 1920s and 1930s some 16½ million people lived on farms in the South and formed more than 40 percent of the population. Since 1940 farmers have been leaving the land at a rate of about one-half million a year, and by 1970 the farm population of the South had dropped to just under 3 million, or only 4 percent of the total population. More than a quarter of the counties of the South, mainly the rural ones, have been losing people steadily since 1940 (Fig. 2).

Black people have continued to leave the region in droves.[3] The massive tide of black migration from the South, which

2. John Fraser Hart, "Loss and Abandonment of Cleared Farm Land in the Eastern United States," *Annals of the Association of American Geographers*, Vol. 58 (1968), pp. 417–40.

3. John Fraser Hart, "The Changing Distribution of the American Negro," *Annals of the Association of American Geographers*, Vol. 50 (1960), pp. 242–66.

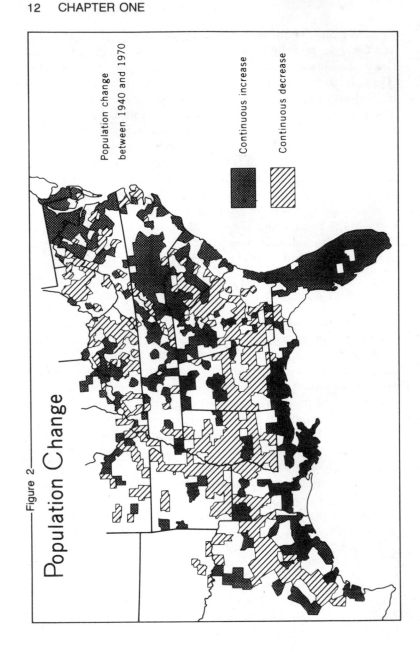

Figure 2

Population Change

Population change
between 1940 and 1970

Continuous increase

Continuous decrease

began during World War I, continued into the 1960s. The level has slowly receded from its crest of 1.6 million in the 1940s, but between 1960 and 1970 approximately 1.38 million Negroes, more than the total population of Atlanta, left the South and moved to cities in other parts of the nation. Most of the white people who left their farms in the South have remained in the region and moved to nearby cities, but only two types of areas have managed to attract significant numbers of migrants: (1) recreation, resort, and retirement areas in the mountains and along the coast, especially peninsular Florida, which alone received more than one million new residents during the decade; and (2) booming metropolitan areas such as Washington, Houston, Dallas, Miami, and Atlanta, each of which has had a growth rate higher than 37 percent for the decade (Table 3).

Although many parts of the South have experienced heavy outmigration, the region as a whole has maintained roughly the same proportion of the nation's population that it had at the time of the Civil War. Each census since 1870 has shown that a third of the nation's people live in the South. The 1970 Census of Population found 63 million people, or just over 30 percent of the national total. The sixteen states of the South lost a grand total of one Congressman between 1940 and 1970, although the corner states gained representation while the middle states lost representation. Virginia added one, Maryland added two, Texas added three, and Florida shot from six to fifteen congressmen. North Carolina lost one, Arkansas lost three, and Oklahoma and a whole block of the middle states (West Virginia, Kentucky, Tennessee, Mississippi, and Alabama) each lost two.

Because of a traditionally high birth rate the population of the South has continued to grow despite heavy outmigration, but the vital rates of the region appear to be converging with those of the nation. The crude birth rate per thousand persons in 1960, for example, was 24.6 in the South and 23.4 in the nation, a difference of 1.2, but by 1970, this figure had dropped to 18.2 in the South and 17.5 in the nation, a difference of only 0.7. The crude death rate in 1970, 9.5 per thou-

TABLE 3. Population of twenty largest urbanized areas

	Thousands of persons		Percentage change
	1970	1960	
Washington, D.C.-Md., Va.	2,481	1,808	37.2
St. Louis, Mo.-Ill.	1,883	1,668	12.9
Houston, Tex.	1,678	1,139	47.3
Baltimore, Md.	1,580	1,419	11.3
Dallas, Tex.	1,339	932	43.6
Miami, Fla.	1,220	853	43.0
Atlanta, Ga.	1,173	768	52.7
Cincinnati, Ohio-Ky.	1,111	994	11.8
New Orleans, La.	962	845	13.8
San Antonio, Tex.	773	642	20.3
Louisville, Ky.-Ind.	739	607	21.9
Fort Worth, Tex.	677	503	34.7
Norfolk-Portsmouth, Va.	668	508	31.6
Memphis, Tenn.-Miss.	664	545	21.9
Fort Lauderdale-Hollywood, Fla.	614	320	91.8
Birmingham, Ala.	558	521	7.1
Jacksonville, Fla.	530	379	39.9
St. Petersburg, Fla.	495	325	52.4
Nashville-Davidson, Tenn.	448	347	29.3
Richmond, Va.	417	333	24.9

sand persons, was the same in the South as in the nation; so the falling birth rate lowered the crude rate of natural increase in the South to within one person per thousand of the national rate.

LAND OF SMALL TOWNS

Although the urban population of the South has been growing rapidly in recent years, the South remains predominantly an area of small towns (Table 2). Most of the major cities which serve the region lie around its edges, not within it (Fig. 3). The

U.S. Bureau of the Census uses three different definitions in reporting the size of the population of each major city. The urban place is the incorporated city, and it includes no one who lives outside the city limits; it is too small. The Standard Metropolitan Statistical Area (SMSA) consists of an entire county, or a group of entire counties, and it includes a considerable number of farmers and other rural people who live beyond the built-up city; it is too large. Geographers prefer to use population figures for the urbanized area, which is defined as the central city and the closely settled territory around it; this is the city as most of us perceive it.

In 1970 the South had eight urbanized areas with more than a million people, but only Atlanta was truly within the South (Table 3). Nine urbanized areas had one-half million to one million people, but only Memphis and Birmingham were in the South. Nashville, Richmond, and Charlotte, N.C., were the next largest urbanized areas in the South, but Charlotte had

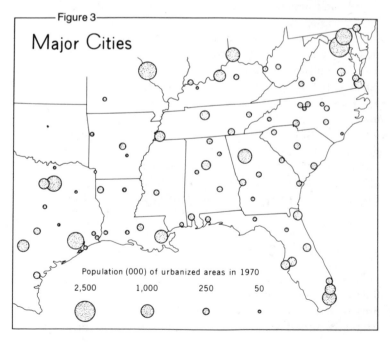

Figure 3

Major Cities

Population (000) of urbanized areas in 1970

2,500   1,000   250   50

only 280,000 people in 1970, and no other city within the South had as many as a quarter of a million people. The most characteristic urban place in the South is the small town of 1 to 10 thousand people, of which the region has far more than its share of the national total (Table 2).

Despite the paucity of major metropolitan centers, the urban population of the South is growing rapidly, from less than 10 million people in 1920, when it was only 28 percent of the total population, to more than 30 million in 1960 and more than 40 million in 1970. In 1970, 65 percent of the people of the South lived in urban areas, as against 74 percent of the people of the nation as a whole (Table 2).

Much of the urban growth of the South is related to the expansion of industry (Fig. 16). The region's share of the nation's production workers in manufacturing has grown from 16 percent in 1920 to 26 percent in 1967, from less than 1½ to well over 3½ million. Industrial growth has been based largely on the manufacture of consumer goods using abundant local supplies of labor, raw materials, and power. The importance of such local raw materials as cotton and wood is demonstrated by the fact that almost half the manufacturing labor force is employed in plants which produce textiles, apparel, lumber, furniture, paper, and related products, and less than a quarter is engaged in metal work and the manufacture of machinery.

The South is richly supplied with oil, gas, coal, and water power. The oil and gas wells of Texas, Louisiana, and Oklahoma caused these three states to rank first, second, and sixth in total value of mineral production in 1970 (Fig. 11). Together they produced more than 12½ billion dollars worth of minerals, or about two-fifths of the national total, including two-thirds of the nation's oil and four-fifths of its natural gas.

West Virginia ranked 4th in total value of mineral production, Kentucky 9th, Virginia 19th, and Alabama 21st, mainly on the basis of coal mined from the enormous Appalachian field. The three northern states produced more than 300 million tons of coal, or about one-half the national total, and Alabama added another 20 million tons. In addition to the power minerals, the mining industry of the South also produces significant amounts of iron ore in Alabama, bauxite in Arkansas, rock phosphate in Florida and Tennessee, and salt and sulfur along the Gulf Coast of Texas and Louisiana.

THE SOUTHERN WAY OF LIFE

The South has a strong regional sense of identity which is based in large part on traditional patterns of living, the so-called Southern way of life. Closer contact with the rest of the nation is rapidly blurring some of the more pronounced idiosyncracies which once characterized the region, but a number are still quite marked, especially in the smaller towns and the countryside. Although this Southern way of life has many facets, seven seem especially worthy of brief mention: (1) a predominantly native-born Protestant population, (2) a distinctive regional diet, (3) strong class distinctions which are not based on income, (4) an aristocratic tradition, (5) the inferior status of Negroes, (6) a talent for self-deception, and (7) the Solid South.

The majority of the people of the South are *native-born Protestants*. In 1970 the region had only 2.8 million first and second generation Americans, less than Greater New York alone; well over half were Spanish-Americans in Texas or Cubans in Florida (Table 2). Furthermore, the South has very few Catholics, apart from the Cajuns of Louisiana and the Spanish-Americans of Texas, and almost no Jews. The Jews of the South, however, have been far more important than their numbers would suggest. Almost every southern community has its small group of economically and civically prominent Jews, many of whom are descended from peddlers who settled down and established businesses for themselves here in the late 1800s. The South has owed a great deal of its scant economic organization to the acumen, enterprise, and enlightened, self-interested civic-mindedness which these people have displayed for three or four generations.

The *diet* of the South is another one of its distinctive features. This is the only section of the nation in which people eat significant quantities of field corn. Some of the corn is ground into meal and baked into cornbread or fried as "hush puppies." Some is leached in lye and made into "hominy." The kernels of hominy may be fried whole, or they may be ground into flinty, pinhead-sized particles and boiled as "hominy grits" (or just plain "grits"), which is standard breakfast fare in many Southern homes and restaurants.

The diet is heavy in fats and fried foods, such as "Southern fried chicken." Chicken and pork, rather than beef, are the staple meats, and rice often supplants potatoes as a starch. Hot rolls or biscuits are considered a necessity with any meal, and iced tea is the standard summer beverage. Mayonnaise is often used where people in other parts of the country would use butter or margarine.

The Southern diet has a number of distinctive foods which are seldom eaten in other parts of the nation, including okra, black-eyed peas, sweet potatoes, and "salad greens" (which means the leaves of plants such as pokeweed, collards, turnips, kale, rape, or spinach); salad greens are prepared by lengthy boiling. The "pot likker" in which the greens are boiled, usually with a piece of fat meat, is considered a great delicacy.

In recent years the distinctive diet of the South has been distributed fairly widely in Northern cities under the guise of "soul food," but in the South it is eaten by black and white alike.

The *strong class distinctions* of the South, which are not based entirely on monetary values, are often confusing to the rest of a nation which bases its class distinctions almost entirely upon income. In most of the rest of the United States you can tell the worth of a man by the amount of money he makes, but in the South that rule is not nearly so valid. A regional reluctance to become preoccupied with economic values may provide much of the explanation for the slow economic growth of the South.

The work ethic never took root in the South. The skill with which Southerners manage to avoid strenuous physical exertion is often mistaken for laziness by those who have never had to try to survive the suffocating, stupefying heat of the long

Southern summer. The traditional costumes of the upper classes, white linen suits for the gentlemen and hoopskirts for the ladies, advertised the fact that their wearers did not have to exert themselves. Ladies used parasols and gloves to protect their dainty skin from the tanning rays of the sun, and a milk-white complexion, rather than the bronzed hide of the "cotton-picking" field hand, was the status symbol of the region.

Class distinctions often are tied to church affiliation; the "best people" are Episcopalians, with Presbyterians, Methodists, and Baptists arrayed behind them in descending order. Many Southerners practice a mild form of "ancestor worship," and maintain a keen interest in kinship relations. The outlander, whether Yankee, foreigner, Roman Catholic, or Jew, never quite arrives, and the Southerner is always slightly startled to have to admit to himself, "That guy's a pretty nice fellow even if he *is* a Yankee."

Despite the fact that few Southerners are able to claim descent from a former plantation owner, the *aristocratic plantation tradition* is still very strong in the South. This tradition emphasizes the virtues of easy-going courtesy and hospitality, the importance of good manners, and a proper respect for the rights and feelings of others. Girls and women act and expect to be treated as ladies, and men and boys are expected to comport themselves as gentlemen. The readiness of Southerners to take the time to be courteous, polite, and thoughtful is often a source of surprise and charm to people in other parts of the nation, where good old-fashioned manners have been abandoned and forgotten in the rush to get ahead.

Outsiders often wonder how Southerners can equate their respect for good manners with their treatment of Negroes. A good part of the answer probably can be found in differences in attitudes toward groups and toward individuals. Southerners feel quite strongly that blacks and whites, as groups, should be segregated in many aspects of their lives, but they treat individual black people as individual human beings, and often develop warm, if paternalistic, relationships with them. Many white people in other parts of the country pay lip service to the ideal of racial integration until it is brought home to them, and quite often reveal considerable prejudice in their everyday dealings with individual black people. Many Northerners preach integration but fail to practice it.

The *inferior status of Negroes* in the South is a carry-over from the plantation tradition. In 1970 this region had slightly less than 12 million Negroes, or just over half of the national total (Table 2). Approximately one Southerner in five was black. Although the South has confronted its racial problems, many Southern whites still accept their black fellow citizens only as servile inferiors. Most Negroes who remain in the South have been forced to remain in a servile status because of the limited educational and economic opportunities which white Southerners have imposed upon them.

One of the problems of the agrarian South was the inability of landlords and tenants to agree on any workable method for producing crops other than cotton and tobacco. A significant key to this problem is the fact that the very idea of landlords and tenants being "bargaining equals" sounds strange to Southern ears. The tenant farmer is a Negro who does as he is told, follows where he is led, and accepts whatever conditions are imposed upon him. One of the great mysteries of Southern history is the question of why Negro tenant farmers never came to an awareness of their bargaining power.

In a very real sense, Southern Negroes can resolve this dilemma and improve their status only by leaving the South. Although the Negro population of the South only increased about 6 percent between 1960 and 1970, the region's share of the nation's Negro population has dropped steadily from 85 percent in 1910 to 53 percent in 1970 (Table 2). In one of the greatest mass migrations in human history, more than 4½ million Negroes moved out of the South to northern cities between 1940 and 1970.

A talent for *self-deception,* which all too often degenerates into pure hypocrisy, is one of the less attractive features of the Southern way of life. Perhaps the most flagrant example may be found in Mississippi, whose citizens used to boast that the state would continue to vote for prohibition as long as a single citizen could still stagger to the polls. Lee County in northeastern Mississippi is famous as "the wettest of the drys."

In a letter dated October 1, 1965, Mr. R. L. Livingston of the Mississippi Liquor Excise Tax Division explained to me that "Mississippi law prohibits the manufacture, possession, and sale of alcoholic beverages other than beer in all of its 82 counties. . . . Since the enforcement of prohibition is a matter of local control, some counties in complete disregard of the prohibition statutes sell distilled spirits openly. That is, liquor is placed on the shelves of the stores selling such commodities in plain view of persons entering the business and in many cases drinks are served over the bar or in restaurants. . . . Liquor is sold from under the counter or concealed drive-in places in many other counties."

Exclusive of the quantities of moonshine which many citizens claimed to prefer, it was estimated that sales of liquor in Mississippi amounted to around $50 million a year. Nothing loath to latch onto a good thing, the state legislature enacted a "black market" tax which applied only to illegal transactions. Although liquor could not legally be sold in Mississippi, the tax on sales of liquor brought some $4.5 million a year into the state treasury.

On May 21, 1966, Gov. Paul B. Johnson, Jr., signed a bill which legalized the sale of liquor in Mississippi under conditions of local option. On August 14 of that year *The New York Times* reported that 33 of the state's 82 counties had chosen to hold local option elections, 28 had gone "wet," and the "only Mississippians who seemed unhappy with the new law were bootleggers and dedicated churchmen."

Another example of turning a blind eye to the strict enforcement of the law was a business establishment in Athens, Georgia, which became known across the state simply as Effie's. Effie's was near the picturesque old covered bridge on Elm Street about a mile and a half from the University of Georgia campus, and it was "Once," to quote *The Atlanta Journal* upon one of the many occasions when it was closed down for the last time, "a principal recreational facility for the then all-male school." The district attorney said that he had no regrets about enforcing the law when he closed Effie's, but he did agree that a historical marker should be placed in front of the establishment.

It was a bit more surprising to find the April 1961 Monthly Review of the Federal Reserve Bank of Atlanta boasting that "for the second time since the American frontier moved west of the Chattahoochee River, the (Sixth Federal Reserve) District states increased their population at a rate greater than that of the nation," when it is blatantly obvious from the accompanying graphs that virtually all of this growth was concentrated in Florida and Louisiana, and that Georgia, Tennessee, Alabama, and Mississippi were actually growing at a slower than national rate.

Finally, the *Solid South*. In 21 presidential elections, between the end of Reconstruction and 1960, four Southern states—South Carolina, Georgia, Alabama, and Mississippi—were never in the Republican column, while North Carolina and Arkansas each fell from grace only once. Apart from the Hoover-Smith election of 1928, the voters of Virginia, Florida, and Louisiana refused to sample the heady wine of Republicanism until 1952, and the same would have been true of Texas but for the election of 1884. In other words, for 19 consecutive elections, from 1876 until 1948, a block of 10 Southern states could be depended on to vote Democratic. The heart of the Plainsland South remained loyal to this tradition even in the Eisenhower-Nixon sweep of 1956 (Fig. 18).

A different kind of Solid South emerged from the 1972 election (Fig. 19). Its origins can be traced back to the 1948 election, when four Southern states gave their votes to the States' Rights party rather than to the Democratic party. It grew in 1964 when Goldwater was not supported by the traditional strongholds of Republicanism, and he was able to carry only six states (five in the South—Louisiana, Mississippi, Alabama, Georgia, and South Carolina—in addition to his home state of Arizona). In 1968 the heart of the South turned to George C. Wallace, but in 1972 it went to Nixon and Agnew in truly astonishing fashion (Fig. 19). The standard bearers of the Republican party received more than seventy percent of the vote in most of the Plainsland South in a striking reversal of the 1956 vote.

WHERE DOES THE SOUTH BEGIN?

The Bureau of the Census divides the United States into four major regions: Northeast, North Central, South, and West. A statistical overview which depends heavily upon Census materials is virtually compelled to accept the Census definition of the South as a block of 16 states, although this definition is scarcely tenable from a geographic point of view. Geographic boundaries do not respect state lines. As Lyndon B. Johnson demonstrated so colorfully, when he raised his sights from the Senate to the White House, western Texas is not part of the South but of the West. The same is true of most of Oklahoma. But the southern part of Missouri, a state which is not often considered Southern, is part of the South, as are bits of southern Illinois and southern Indiana.

The South has no sharp, clear-cut, and generally accepted boundaries. The location of the boundaries of any region is determined by the definition of the region, and no one ever has or ever will be able to come up with a completely satisfactory definition of the South. In the East the Mason-Dixon Line is usually considered the northern boundary of the South, but both Maryland and Delaware are more properly considered part of Megalopolis (the chain of cities which sprawls from Boston to Washington) than of the South. Perhaps the Potomac River is a more fitting boundary than the line which Messrs. Mason and Dixon so carefully surveyed, but even northern Virginia is being drawn ever more tightly and closely into the orbit of the national capital, and the area is losing much of its Southern flavor.

The boundary between North and South becomes quite indistinct as it crosses West Virginia, probably somewhere north of Charleston and south of Clarksburg. Some of southeastern Ohio undoubtedly is part of the Appalachian South, and the Ohio River is merely a boundary of convenience. The glaciated hills of southern Indiana and southern Illinois are part of the South, and so are the Ozark uplands of southern Missouri and eastern Oklahoma. The western edge of the South is marked fairly closely by the foot of the escarpment which rises to the west of the Blackland Prairie of eastern Texas.

The South itself is an area of great diversity, an area which contains within itself differences as great or greater than those which distinguish it from other sections of the nation. One of the most important is the difference between hills and plains. The northern part of the South is predominantly hilly to mountainous, with a few level to rolling areas, whereas the southern part is a vast plainsland with a few areas of rougher topography (Fig. 5). The Border Hills of the north are quite different from the vast southern plainsland that was once the Cotton Belt (Fig. 6).

2 Cotton Belt No Longer

The great triad of the South, for more than a century, was cotton, plainsland, and Negroes. The traditional Cotton Belt, as defined by O. E. Baker during the period of peak cotton acreage, occupied much of the vast plainsland stretching along the Atlantic and Gulf coasts from Long Island to the Rio Grande. The Plainsland South, which is essentially the two areas known to geologists as the Coastal Plain and Piedmont physiographic provinces, was the home of two-thirds of the nation's Negroes, including almost all of those who lived on farms.

The triad has been broken since the end of World War II. Between 1940 and 1970 Negroes left the South at a rate of about 12 thousand a month. The plainsland is still there, but cotton has shrunk to the status of just another crop (Fig. 4). It has remained important on the land best suited to its production, but the men who farm the old Cotton Belt have been experimenting with exciting new ideas on land which once grew mainly cotton.

The Plainsland South, of course, was never one great field of cotton. Much of the land is heavily wooded (Fig. 7), and crops such as tobacco, rice, soybeans, and peanuts are more important than cotton in some areas. Tobacco is a major crop in eastern North and South Carolina, rice in eastern Arkansas, and soybeans along the Mississippi River bottomlands (Fig. 4).

25

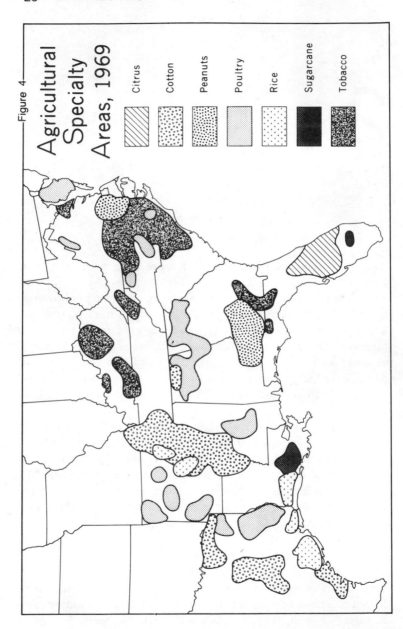

Figure 4

Agricultural Specialty Areas, 1969

Citrus

Cotton

Peanuts

Poultry

Rice

Sugarcane

Tobacco

About half of the nation's peanuts are grown in southeastern Alabama and southwestern Georgia; another major peanut area is in southeastern Virginia and northeastern North Carolina.

THE SEARCH FOR A CROP

The Englishmen who settled at Jamestown in 1607 soon realized that they were not going to find quick riches in the New World, and they turned to farming as a means of livelihood. Casting around for a cash crop to export, they experimented with growing grapes, hemp, flax, indigo, and all manner of exotic fruits, nuts, and spices. The first real breakthrough was made in 1612, when John Rolfe planted some tobacco seed. Tobacco was an almost instant success when it was landed in Europe, and the crop became the stable export of the Virginia and Maryland colonies. Shipments rose from 20 thousand pounds in 1618 to 500 thousand pounds in 1627 and 28 million pounds in the 1680s.

The crop was grown on large plantations scattered along the shores of Chesapeake Bay and its numerous estuaries. No towns of any size developed in this area, for each planter shipped his crop from his own wharf. The plantations had to be large, for tobacco exhausted the soil in a short time. The tobacco fields were usually turned over to other crops after three years or so, and new land was cleared for tobacco. Much of the heavy field work was done by indentured servants, whose passage to the New World had been paid by the tobacco planter in return for their agreement to work for him for a specified number of years. The indentured servants were free men as soon as they had worked out their period of indenture, commonly seven years, and they began growing tobacco in competition with their former masters. All of the land along the coast was soon taken up, and settlers began to head for the "back country" where they became subsistence farmers in wilderness clearings.

The early settlers in South Carolina, which was founded as an English outpost against the Spanish in Florida, also cast around for a cash crop. After some experimentation, they learned that indigo did well on the sandy uplands, and that rice was an excellent crop for the steaming swamps along the rivers and seacoast. The problem of supplying labor for the unpleasant work in the rice paddies was solved by importing large numbers of Negro slaves from Africa. Many of the rice plantations were so large that planters could afford to entrust them to overseers and live in Charleston, which was the fourth largest city in early America (and remained the eleventh largest city in the United States as late as 1850).

Despite the importance of tobacco in Maryland and Virginia, and rice and indigo in South Carolina, the frontier of settlement remained close to the Atlantic Coast for almost two centuries. In 1790 the western wilderness lay less than 100 miles west of the Georgia-South Carolina line, and then suddenly, within 50 years, settlers had spread right across the South into eastern Texas. This explosion of settlement was triggered when a Connecticut Yankee named Eli Whitney developed a vastly improved type of cotton gin in 1793.[1]

Around 1800 British textile mills were hungry for cotton. Many of the early innovations of the Industrial Revolution had been improvements in textile machinery, which enabled the mills to outstrip their traditional sources of raw materials. Heretofore cotton had not been a profitable crop because of the tedious and costly process of separating the seeds from the clinging fiber, but now a single slave using Whitney's gin could clean 50 pounds of cotton a day. Southern agriculture was revolutionized, as cotton production shot from almost nothing in 1790 to 100 thousand bales in 1800, and more than 5 million in 1860.

GOOD CLIMATE AND POOR SOILS

One of the greatest natural assets of the Cotton Belt is its climate. Winters are short and comparatively mild, with occa-

1. C. S. Aiken, "An Examination of the Role of the Eli Whitney Cotton Gin in the Origin of the United States Cotton Regions," *Proceedings,* Association of American Geographers, Vol. 3 (1971), pp. 5–9.

sional brief spells of severe weather. The temperature averages between 40° and 50° in January, and the coldest nights seldom drop lower than 10°, although most places have recorded below-zero temperatures at one time or another. Danger of frost is over by the middle or end of March, and the first frost in fall does not come until late October or early November, thus giving a frost-free growing season of seven months or more.

Summers are long and hot. July averages around 80°, and the mercury is almost guaranteed to break 100° every summer, although it seldom goes much higher. Summer nights, as well as summer days, are hot and oppressively humid. The summer sky is flecked with fleecy clouds, like giant bolls of cotton, which often build into angry thunderheads and unleash torrential showers. A single summer thunderstorm may pound the earth with 6 inches or more of torrential rain.

The southeastern United States, which has an average annual rainfall of 40 inches or more, is one of the wetter parts of the world. In addition to its heavy summer thundershowers, this area often receives heavy rainfall from autumn hurricanes. Nevertheless, short droughts occur almost every year, and many farmers have learned that they can increase their crop yields appreciably by using supplemental irrigation even in years with normal rainfall.

Because of its mild temperatures and heavy rainfall, the Cotton Belt suffers from one of Nature's paradoxes: those areas which have the best climate for farming often have the poorest soils. Chemical plant foods break down quickly in a hot moist climate, and are rapidly leached out by the heavy rainfall, leaving only the insoluble residues. With a few notable exceptions, the soils of the Cotton Belt are no better than mediocre for farming purposes.

Furthermore, the low inherent productivity of the soil has been greatly reduced by the treatment it has received. Continuous production of row crops has exposed it to regular battering by heavy rains, and serious erosion problems have resulted. One of the world's most spectacular erosion gullies, near Columbus, Georgia, was started by water dripping from a barn roof; within 50 years it had reached a depth of 200 feet and covered an area of almost 5 square miles.

In recent years, however, many of the more serious gully erosion problems have been corrected, largely through the herculean efforts of the Soil Conservation Service. Many farmers in the South now practice contour plowing and strip cropping, use improved crop rotations, and plant cover crops to protect their soil. Thousands of hillsides have low earthen terraces which do not interfere with cultivation, but slow down rapid runoff water and guide it to a safe disposal.

Cotton is hard on the land, and several methods have been used in the South to combat the problem of soil exhaustion. In the early days the land was simply abandoned when it lost its fertility. There always seemed to be plenty of cheap virgin land in the west, and the cotton planter took his slaves to open new land there, while the abandoned cotton land in the east reverted to scrubby pine forest.

Many of the cotton farmers who remained in the east practiced a system of shifting cultivation, or "forest fallow." After 8 to 10 years of cultivation the land was allowed to revert to woodland, and it had regained some of its former fertility when it was cleared once again in 30 to 50 years. Such a system, of course, required the farmer to have about five times as much land as he was actually cultivating. At any given time only a small fraction of his land was actually growing crops, while the remainder was wooded. This is part of the explanation for the high proportion of woodland in many parts of the old Cotton Belt (Fig. 7).

Cotton farmers have also relied heavily on commerical fertilizers to maintain soil fertility. One of the first of these was guano imported from Peru, and in parts of the South "guano" is still the folk name for any commercial fertilizer. Until the Second World War the South consumed more than half of the commercial fertilizer used in the United States and many farmers in the Cotton Belt still put the fertility into the soil in the spring, when they plant their seed, and remove it in the fall when the crop is harvested.

THE PLANTATION SYSTEM

Although the majority of cotton farmers worked their own land and had no slaves, the large slave-holding plantation was one of the more spectacular features of the antebellum South. The planter and his family lived in "the big house," which was seldom quite as fancy as Hollywood would like to have us believe. Close by were "the quarters," a compact group of cabins for the slaves, plus tool and implement sheds, the mule barn, and the blacksmith shop. On all sides were the large fields where gangs of Negro slaves worked under the watchful eye of an overseer. The most efficient plantation units consisted of 900 to 1,000 acres of land worked by 60 to 100 slaves, but many planters owned more than one unit, each of which was managed by its own overseer.

A good field hand, without machinery, could handle no more than 10 to 15 acres of cotton, for much of the work of growing the crop is concentrated into two fairly brief periods. The soil is prepared in late spring, and the seeds are planted in April. Once the young plants have sprouted, the field must be carefully cultivated to get rid of grass and weeds which compete with them. The traditional technique of "chopping" grass and weeds with a hand hoe required large amounts of labor in May, June, and July. The second busy season comes in September when the ripe bolls are picked, and once again large amounts of hand labor were required before the days of mechanical cotton pickers.

Emancipation of the slaves wrought major changes in the old plantation system.[2] The planter still owned the land, but he had no labor to work it; the freed slaves had no land. From this dilemma emerged the infamous system known as sharecropping. The planter provided the land and the tools of production, the sharecropper provided the labor, and they split the cost of seed and fertilizer. Unlike a true tenancy system,

2. These changes have been superbly described and illustrated in Merle C. Prunty, "The Renaissance of the Southern Plantation," *Geographical Review*, Vol. 45 (1955), pp. 459–91.

however, the cropper made no management decisions, for the planter told him when and how to plant, cultivate, pick, and sell the crop, and much of the work was done by gang labor rather than individually.

The large fields of the old plantation were divided into smaller sharecropper subunits of 30 to 40 acres. The old quarters, reminiscent of slavery days, were razed, and new cabins were scattered through the cotton fields, with a cabin on each subunit. Most cropper cabins were little better than rude shacks, cheaply constructed of native lumber, with sheet metal roofs. They were seldom painted, for replacement was cheaper than paint. Many were set on piers of brick or stone, which provided an air space beneath the floor, and had a fairly large front porch with a swing or chairs. The porch often was decorated with potted plants and, in later days, the family washing machine. A bare earthen yard separated the cabin from the cotton fields surrounding it.

The rural landscape had a general air of shabbiness, unkemptness, and neglect. The blistering summer sun beat down on the rain-gullied soil, with its hues of eye-searing red or bright yellow-tan. There were few pastures, and fences were not needed for the cotton fields, nor for the fields in which the cropper grew corn to feed himself, his family, and his mule.

The small towns were little better. Most were merely local service centers, with a small bank, shabby stores, and flyblown restaurants clustering near the county courthouse. Rust-stained metal awnings sagging over the sidewalk provided a bit of shelter from the shimmering summer sun and driving rains. The only factories were cotton gins and other plants which processed local agricultural products. In the countryside, where Negroes comprised up to three-quarters of the population, there was no sharp residential segregation of the races. In the small towns the houses of the white people faced the paved streets, and the unpainted wooden shacks of their Negro servants lined the unpaved back alleys.

Sharecropping involved an intricate system of credit, for often neither planter nor cropper had enough ready capital to cover his share of the cost of farming and living. The cropper expected the planter to provide him with "furnish," i.e., seed, fertilizer, and even food and clothing, which were charged against his share of the crop at the end of the season. Many plantations had their own stores at which croppers were required to make all of their purchases. The planter, in turn, borrowed from his banker, merchant, or dealer when the cropping season opened in the spring, and paid his debts after the crop had been harvested in the fall.

THE SHRINKING COTTON BELT

The importance of cotton, which had dominated much of the Plainsland South between the Civil War and the First World War, began to decline dramatically during the 1920s. Before 1930, for example, more than 40 percent of the cropland harvested in the six states of Arkansas, Louisiana, Mississippi, Alabama, Georgia, and South Carolina had produced cotton, but by 1970 the figure had dropped to 16 percent, and the actual acreage had shrunk from more than 15 million acres to less than 4 million (Table 4). In 1900 these six states produced more than 60 percent of the nation's cotton, but by 1970 they were producing only 40 percent.

Many factors help to account for the striking changes which have taken place. One was the depredations of the boll weevil, an insect which was first noticed in southern Texas in 1894. The female boll weevil lays her eggs in developing cotton bolls. After they hatch out, the larvae destroy the fiber and then fly away to lay more eggs. Between 1909 and 1921, when the growing army of boll weevils had invaded the entire Cotton Belt, it is estimated that they destroyed an average of more than 2 million bales of cotton a year.

Eventually means were found to reduce damage from the boll weevil by destroying its hibernating areas and by spraying the growing cotton plants with insecticides, but the only sure cure was to stop growing cotton and switch to some other crop. In 1919 the good citizens of Enterprise, Alabama, erected a monument to the boll weevil, which had brought them new prosperity when the local farmers were forced to

TABLE 4. Cotton in six Southern states, 1900–1970*

	1970	1960	1950	1940	1930	1920	1910	1900
Thousands of acres	3,918	5,205	10,863	10,559	18,346	16,825	17,689	14,706
Percentage of U.S. total	*35.0*	*35.5*	*40.8*	*46.3*	*42.4*	*49.9*	*55.2*	*60.6*
Thousands of bales	4,179	5,139	5,666	6,130	7,565	6,011	6,575	6,009
Percentage of U.S. total	*41.0*	*36.9*	*36.7*	*53.4*	*51.9*	*52.8*	*61.7*	*63.0*
Bales per acre	1.07	0.99	0.52	0.58	0.41	0.36	0.37	0.41
Thousands of acres of cropland harvested	24,785	23,642	32,002	37,852	36,834	39,882	37,141	33,701
Cotton as a percentage of cropland harvested	15.8	22.0	33.9	27.9	49.8	42.2	47.6	43.6

* Arkansas, Louisiana, Mississippi, Alabama, Georgia, and South Carolina.

switch from cotton to peanuts. (The "world's only monument to a pest," an enormous model of a boll weevil held proudly aloft by a Greek goddess, has enjoyed a rather less than prosperous history. The insect portion was stolen in 1953 and had to be replaced; in 1974 the entire statue was stolen, but it was soon found in a roadside ditch near the Army helicopter school at Fort Rucker. This school is now the economic mainstay of the town—perhaps the boll weevil statue should be replaced by a statue of a helicopter).

A second, and related, factor in reducing cotton acreage was the loss of Negro labor. Cotton farmers had been slow to develop new machinery and labor-saving methods, for they had relied on an abundant Negro labor force for the demanding chores of chopping and picking cotton. Negroes first began to leave the South in large numbers during the First World War, when northern industrial centers were cut off from their traditional supply of unskilled workers from central and eastern Europe. Large numbers of Negroes have continued to migrate out of the South ever since, and the growing shortage of labor has forced many cotton farmers to stop growing cotton or to convert to the use of machinery.

A third factor which helped shrink the Cotton Belt was legislation designed to improve the lot of the cotton farmer. The price of cotton was never satisfactory in the interwar years. It tumbled from 35 cents a pound in 1919 to 16 cents in 1920, recovered somewhat in the next few years, and then dropped to an all-time low of only 6 cents a pound in 1931. The falling price of cotton was one of the farm problems which stimulated agitation for agricultural legislation during the 1920s, the agitation which culminated in the Agricultural Adjustment Act of 1933.

This Act, and the legislation which has followed it, has two basic features. Farmers were to be guaranteed a price for their crops, and in return, would reduce the acreage they planted. During the summer of 1933, for example, some 10 million acres of cotton which had already been planted were plowed up under the AAA program of raising prices by limiting production. In subsequent years the Secretary of Agriculture has determined the total acreage of cotton which should be planted in the entire nation. This acreage was then allotted on the basis of their past production, to states, by states to counties, and at the county level, to individual farmers. A farmer was assessed a penalty for exceeding his allotted acreage, but he was guaranteed a price for the crop he grew on it.

Although price supports and acreage controls initially increased farm income, they eventually put many cotton farmers out of business, or reduced them to misery. By concentrating cotton allotments on their best land, cultivating more intensively, and fertilizing more heavily, cotton farmers in the South were able to double their yields per acre between 1930 and 1960, and national cotton production continued to increase. Each increase in production necessitated another cut in acreage, and an ever larger number of cotton farmers found themselves with impossibly small acreage allotments. In the early 1960s, for example, an allotment of 50 acres was considered the absolute minimum for profitable production making use of machinery, yet two-thirds of all cotton producers had mule-sized allotments of less than 15 acres.[3]

The high support price of cotton encouraged producers in other areas to get into the act, under the shelter of the price umbrella which was being held over cotton farmers in the South. The United States, which produced more than half the world's cotton short years ago, was growing little more than a fifth of it in 1970. Even in the United States new areas outside the Cotton Belt have become major producers. Mechanized

3.   Prunty and Aiken have seen fit to quibble with this sentence, but the only counterevidence they have produced is one single agricultural station bulletin from Missouri; Merle C. Prunty and Charles S. Aiken, "The Demise of the Piedmont Cotton Region," *Annals,* Association of American Geographers, Vol. 62 (1972), pp. 283–306, reference on p. 306. I am still inclined to agree with Aiken that "a modern farmer . . . needs to plant between 50 and 250 acres of the fiber to justify ownership of a one-row mechanical picker"; Charles S. Aiken, "The Fragmented Neoplantation: A New Type of Farm Operation in the Southeast," *Southeastern Geographer,* Vol. 11, No. 1 (April, 1971), pp. 43–51, reference on p. 47.

farmers on irrigated land in the West can grow cotton at half the cost in the South, and they can grow two bales to the acre, whereas one is considered good in the old Cotton Belt. In a normal year California alone produces more cotton than Alabama, Georgia, and South Carolina combined.

All cotton producers have suffered from the growing popularity of man-made synthetic fibers, such as rayon, nylon, dacron, orlon, and on and on. Cotton has benefitted from the popularity of denim and corduroy, but the cotton/synthetic consumption ratio in textile mills dropped from 75/25 in 1950 to 40/60 in 1970.

MORE COTTON FROM LESS LAND

Although cotton has lost its former dominance, it is still a major crop in certain parts of the South (Fig. 4). As a general rule, cotton production has become concentrated in the most fertile areas, and in level areas where modern machinery and equipment can be used efficiently. The process of readjustment would probably have been more rapid but for the fact that acreage allotments tended to "freeze" traditional geographical patterns of production; the man who had an allotment, however small, has treasured it even though he has been unable to use it effectively. One ingenious cotton planter even went so far as to claim an income tax deduction in 1973 for a business loss, when the government reduced the value of his allotment by suspending the customary penalties on cotton grown in excess of the allotted acreage; his claim was disallowed by the Internal Revenue Service and the Tax Court.

A brisk business sprang up in the buying, selling, and leasing of allotment rights as soon as the regulations permitted such practices. A man with an undersized allotment could rent or sell his right to a neighbor and switch to some other kind of farming, or even take a job in town; alternatively, he might use his allotment as a home base for putting together an operation of adequate size by buying or renting allotments from others. A farmer who owns part of his land and rents the rest is a part-owner farmer. It seems quite unnecessary to coin such fanciful terms as "multiple tenancy" and "fragmented neo-plantation" to describe part-owner farm operations. Part-ownership has been a well-known technique of enlarging a farm operation without tying up large amounts of capital in land for more than a generation, although it apparently had "not been examined or recognized" by Prunty and his colleagues "until quite recently."[4]

To an increasing degree, successful cotton farmers in the South are using the full range of modern methods in science and technology to raise their yields and lower their costs. They apply lime and fertilizers to maintain the fertility of their soil, herbicides to control weeds, pesticides to control insects, and defoliants to prepare the plants for machine harvesting. They are developing crop rotations with new field and forage crops, and are diversifying their operations by introducing livestock.

Machines are rapidly replacing hand labor, for a man with proper machinery can handle 10 times as much cotton as a man without. It is usually estimated that at least 100 acres of cotton land and at least 100 bales of cotton are necessary if a fully mechanized farm is to be successful. More than two-thirds of the cotton crop is now being picked mechanically, and even aircraft have been pressed into service. In summer the sky of many cotton districts is full of low-flying planes spewing various chemicals onto the growing crop. The city of Clarksdale, Mississippi, for example, alone boasts 14 crop-dusting outfits which operate up to 100 or more planes.

One of the more bizarre techniques for increasing cotton yields is skip-row planting. As their acreage allotments have dwindled, cotton farmers have been cramming their rows closer together in the fields and plants closer together in the rows. Eventually the plants were so tightly packed that only those on the outside rows had enough light and air to enable them to attain their full growth. By planting two rows and skipping two, some farmers have been able to spread their allotments over double the acreage, make every row an outside row, and thus increase their yields up to 50 percent.

4. Prunty and Aiken, op. cit., footnote 3, p. 292.

COTTON DISTRICTS TODAY

Today the old Cotton Belt has shrunk to only two major cotton producing districts (Fig. 4). The largest is the alluvial bottomlands of the Mississippi River and its tributaries, an area widely known as the Delta, which reaches from southern Illinois to northeastern Louisiana (Fig. 6). The land is flat and has poor natural drainage, but the dark-colored soils are rich in organic materials and prove extremely fertile when adequately drained and protected from flooding.

The danger of floods and the expense of clearing its thick hardwood forests delayed the settlement of most of the Delta until well after the Civil War, and the clearance of forest land for agricultural purposes continues even today. The rich alluvial bottomlands, despite their fertility, have spawned only one major metropolitan center. Memphis, which has become one of the world's leading cotton markets, overlooks the Mississippi floodplain from its perch atop the Chickasaw Bluffs, the last high ground near the river north of Vicksburg, nearly two hundred miles to the south.

Acreage restrictions and labor shortages prevent Delta farmers from placing all of their land in cotton, and they have experimented with a variety of other crops. Soybeans have become the most important second crop in most of the Delta, for they fit in well with cotton cultivation and find a ready market at a good price. Rice is a major crop on large, highly mechanized, and extensively irrigated farms in eastern Arkansas. Rice is grown on loessial terraces whose soils are underlain by heavy plastic clay. This clay prevents loss of water by percolation when the fields are flooded.

The second largest cotton district in the South is the Blackland Prairie of eastern Texas, which has rich soils derived from limestone (Figs. 4 and 6). Cotton is grown on the deeper soils of the more level areas, and winter grains and forage crops on the poorer sloping land. Farmers in this area have placed greater emphasis on grazing and livestock in recent years. Beef cattle numbers have been increasing rapidly, and the Blackland Prairie has become the nucleus of one of the most important livestock producing districts in the contemporary South.

The Blackland Prairie is also the most highly urbanized area in the South, with major metropolitan centers at crossing points on the rivers which diagonal southeastward across it (Table 3 and Fig. 3). More than 2 million people live in the Dallas/Fort Worth conurbation to the north, on the Trinity River, and Waco on the Brazos has nearly 120 thousand. Austin, on the Colorado River, was specifically selected as the capital of Texas, and has grown with the state to pass the quarter-million mark. San Antonio to the south, formerly the northern outpost of Spanish power, and the cradle of Texas liberty, has a population of 3/4 million people.

FORMER COTTON DISTRICTS

Cotton is still grown on a greatly reduced scale in five former producing districts where once it was the major crop: the Inner Coastal Plain of the Carolinas and Georgia; the Piedmont of the Carolinas and Georgia; the Black Belt of Alabama and Mississippi; the limestone valleys of northern Alabama; and scattered areas on the plains of southern Texas.

The limestone valleys of northern Alabama, drained by the Tennessee and Coosa rivers, are the most important of the lesser cotton producing districts. The soils of this area are highly productive, and the level to gently rolling land is well suited to mechanized farm operations. It lies outside the Plainsland South and has a comparatively small number of Negroes except on the larger farms. This area has great potential for livestock because its soil can produce good pastures, and feed grains can be imported by barge on the Tennessee River. Many local farmers have gone into the broiler business, and the area is dotted with poultry houses. Electrical power from the TVA has stimulated considerable industrial development here, including the Space Age city of Huntsville.

Most of the former cotton producing districts in the South have gone out of the cotton business because their costs of production have been higher than those in the new low-cost

districts in the West and in other parts of the world.[5] A few
farmers in the older districts still grow cotton, apparently because they do not know how to do anything else nearly so well;
but they have been reluctant to adopt or unable to afford
modern techniques and equipment, and their costs keep spi-
ralling upward. Gin operators have been caught in the same
spiral, and the smarter ones have been scrambling pathetically
to protect their investments by branching out into other lines
of business.

It is a bit sad that most geographers in the South have not
been able to develop an objective and dispassionate view of
the region, because it could offer a splendid laboratory for
studying the birth and death pangs of agricultural regions.
Acreage allotments certainly have frozen cotton production in
certain areas long after it should have been allowed to die, but
moribund agricultural regions have also been maintained by
such conservative elements of the infrastructure as processing
and marketing facilities, and the accumulated know-how of
local people.

A farmer must understand the techniques of production.
Would you, for instance, be able to distinguish boll weevils
from June bugs, or know when and how to plant, transplant,
top, sucker, and prime tobacco, or how to castrate a steer, or
how to rig up a block and tackle to help out a cow that was
having trouble calving? What is the right kind of fertilizer?
Would the local banker be willing to lend you enough money
to buy a self-propelled combine, or a mechanical cotton har-
vester, or a carload of feeder cattle?

A successful farmer must have know-how, the right advice,
and a source of working capital. He also needs the right structures and facilities for producing, processing, and selling his

5. It is absurd to try to dismiss this fact on the fatuous grounds
that producers in high-cost districts can remain competitive if they
are efficient, because a high-cost district, by definition, is one in which
most producers are not efficient, and costs are not high in districts
where most producers are efficient; Prunty and Aiken, op. cit., footnote 3, p. 296.

goods: fences to separate crops and livestock; shelters for crops, stock, tools, and machinery; on- and off-farm process-ing facilities such as cotton gins, tobacco barns, packing plants, and creameries to prepare the goods for market; tobacco warehouses, grain elevators, stockyards, and auction markets where they can be sold.[6]

The production of a given agricultural commodity may be maintained in an area long after it should have been aban-doned because the local people have too great an investment in the know-how and facilities necessary for producing it; the former cotton producing districts of the South are an excellent example. Conversely, the lack of such know-how and facilities may thwart the development of new forms of production; per-haps the failure of the livestock industry of the South to live up to its much publicized potential is an example. Facilities are not always a critical factor, however; soybean production in the South has increased enormously in recent years because the crop is relatively easy to produce with traditional farm machinery, the beans can be pressed like cotton seed, and the price has been right.

6. The role of man-made structures in rural areas is discussed at length in John Fraser Hart, *The Look of the Land* (Englewood Cliffs, N.J.: Prentice-Hall, 1975).

3 New Uses for Old Lands

The concentration of cotton production in the most favored sections of the old Cotton Belt has released a large amount of land for other uses. Much of this land is of mediocre quality, and some of it—no one knows how much—simply lies idle. Many landowners, however, have been experimenting with new ways of making their land productive, and three of these have become important in certain parts of the region. The first is a growing emphasis on forestry, especially in relation to the pulp and paper industry. The second is the production of a variety of specialty crops, such as peanuts, vegetables, and tree crops. The third is an increased emphasis on livestock, such as cattle and poultry, and the development of pasture and hay lands.

THE QUALITY OF THE LAND

Although the quality of the land varies enormously within the old Cotton Belt, four major land types can be recognized (Fig. 6). The Delta, which is the alluvial plain of the Mississippi River and its major tributaries, stretches some 500 miles southward from the mouth of the Ohio River to the coastal marshlands along the Gulf of Mexico. Although the land is naturally flat and swampy, it becomes extremely fertile with proper drainage and flood protection. Much of this area is still cotton country, with soybeans an important secondary crop.

The other three major land types are arranged in belts more or less parallel to the coast. The innermost belt, which has been identified as the Piedmont Land Type, includes the loess bluffs just east of the Mississippi alluvial plain, the Black Belt of Mississippi and Alabama, the inner Coastal Plain of Alabama and Georgia, and the Piedmont proper, from east central Alabama to Washington, D. C. These areas boasted the most productive farm land in the Plainsland South until settlement pushed westward as far as the Blackland Prairie of Texas, and before the Delta had been drained. The Piedmont Land Type has a few isolated hilly areas, but for the most part topography poses no serious obstacles to agriculture (Fig. 5).

The other two land types generally have less fertile and less productive farm land. On the Atlantic slope the rolling Sandy Lands lie between the Piedmont and the coastal Flatwoods (Fig. 6). The Sandy Lands, which have light-colored, acid soil, widen out in the west to include much of eastern Mississippi, western Louisiana, and eastern Texas. The low-lying, poorly drained coastal Flatwoods have extensive areas of swampland and marsh, including the famous Dismal and Okefenokee swamps. Most parts of the Sandy Lands and the coastal Flat-

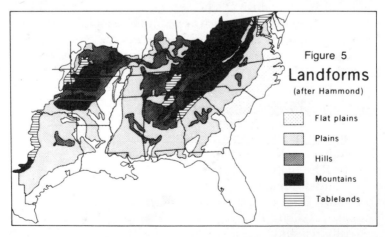

Figure 5
Landforms
(after Hammond)

Flat plains

Plains

Hills

Mountains

Tablelands

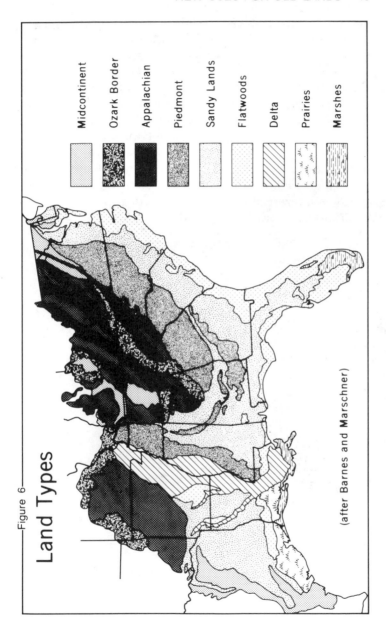

Figure 6

Land Types

Midcontinent
Ozark Border
Appalachian
Piedmont
Sandy Lands
Flatwoods
Delta
Prairies
Marshes

(after Barnes and Marschner)

woods have soils which are poor even by Southern standards, and much of the land simply is not worth farming.

These two poor land types are covered by the vast southern pine forest which reaches from eastern Texas to Chesapeake Bay (Fig. 7). The piney woods have a mixture of longleaf and slash pines, with an understory of scrub oak and gum trees, and a ground cover of palmetto scrub and wiregrass. Stream bottomlands and other poorly drained areas carry stands of cypress, blackgum, and tupelo. Inferior hardwoods sometimes become dominant on better drained uplands where the pines have been cleared. Away from coastal areas the piney woods give way to a forest of loblolly and shortleaf pine, with some oak, hickory, and other hardwoods.

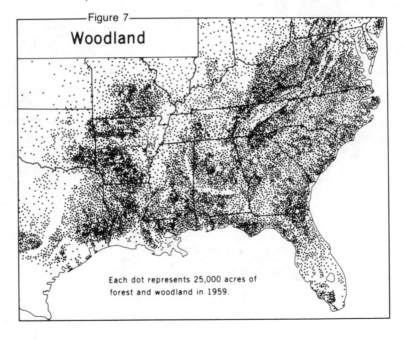

Figure 7

Woodland

Each dot represents 25,000 acres of forest and woodland in 1959.

FARM WOODLANDS

In the past trees have been little more than weeds for many farmers in the old Cotton Belt, and to a certain extent this is true even today. Trees had to be cleared from the land before it could grow cotton and corn. They quickly recolonized fields which had been abandoned in the cycle of shifting cultivation. The new growth of trees had to be cleared once again before the land could be returned to crop production.

The U.S. Department of Agriculture has recognized the role of trees in Southern farming by subsidizing two kinds of forest operations. In many Southern counties a farmer can go to one office in the county courthouse and obtain financial aid to clear trees from one part of his farm, so that he can plant crops on it. In the office next door he can obtain financial aid to plant trees on another part of the same farm.

More than one real estate operator, with a good knowledge of forestry, has made a pretty penny for himself by capitalizing on the attitude of Southern farmers toward trees. The operator bought a farm for a song, because it was wooded. After cutting and selling the trees he could usually sell the farm at a considerable profit because the land was cleared.

Much of the farm woodland in the old Cotton Belt has been essentially wasteland, for the farmer knew little and cared less about good forest management practices. In 1953 the U.S. Forest Service estimated that only a third of the commercial forest land of the old Cotton Belt was well stocked, and a quarter—more than 25 million acres, an area almost as large as the state of Pennsylvania—was stocked poorly or not at all. The woods were commonly burned off each spring to kill the weeds and undergrowth, thus providing scanty forage for cattle and hogs which were turned loose to rustle for themselves.

Almost every county had one or more small portable sawmills, and there were a few larger ones, but for the most part farmers received only a minor portion of their income from the sale of forest products. This situation was changed after the Second World War when the constant-dollar value of the southern pine stumpage price—the price paid for standing timber—more than doubled.

The lumber industry continued to change during the 1960s. Large, new, efficient, modern mills replaced the old portable sawmills, which had been small and inefficient. In Alabama, for example, the number of sawmills dropped from 3,030 in 1946 to 555 in 1962 to 323 in 1971, but their average capacity increased fivefold. Many of the new mills had chipping head-rigs, which produce less sawdust and more chips. Chips from sawmills have become increasingly important as raw materials for pulp mills.

Improvements in peeling equipment have encouraged the production of plywood veneer from small southern pine logs, and the softwood plywood industry expanded rapidly in the South during the 1960s. The first mill was opened in Fordyce, Arkansas, late in 1963; only nine years later the South had no less than 53 plants which produced 20 percent of the nation's softwood plywood.

FOREST MANAGEMENT

Some Southern farmers, after they had learned that they could haul a load of logs to the sawmill and receive a good and fairly well established price for it, began to realize that trees can be just as much a crop as cotton, and they have taken a keen interest in effective woodland management. Foresters employed by state and Federal forest services and the forest industry have provided a wide range of professional advice, and plant breeders are trying to develop taller, straighter, better trees with greater diameter and less taper. Much land too poor to farm, as well as some better land, has been con-verted into productive forest land under programs of sus-tained yield tree farming, but an enormous amount of im-provement is still necessary. In 1971, for example, Alabama alone had an estimated 10 million acres of potentially good pine forest land that carried only small and misshapen hard-wood trees of little or no commercial value.

Natural regeneration of southern pines takes only two or three years if enough seed trees are available, but the process can be expedited by scarifying the ground to expose the min-eral soil. The young trees grow very quickly. A young loblolly pine, for example, may grow two or three feet in a year, reach 35 feet in 15 years, and attain saw timber size within 40 years.

An acre of southern pine forest ought to produce around 500 board feet of saw timber, or more than a cord of pulpwood, each year. When it is 12 to 20 years old, the stand is thinned for pulpwood, fence posts, and the like, to enable the remaining trees to grow more rapidly. A second thinning yields good poles and pilings and at 40 to 60 years the mature forest is ready to be cut for saw timber. Tree harvesting has become increasingly mechanized, with giant hydraulic shears that nip off the trees at ground level, feller-bunchers, mechanical loaders, and rubber-tired skidders.

The forest may be harvested on an even-aged or an all-aged basis. The trees in an even-aged forest are all of about the same age, and they are felled at the same time, with the exception of a well-distributed few which are left as seed trees. The all-aged forest has trees of many ages and sizes. The larger trees are felled as they reach maturity, so cuttings are made frequently, perhaps every five years or less. Although an all-aged forest provides a more regular income, it also runs greater risk of fire damage, because it always has a certain number of young trees.

SETTIN' THE WOODS ON FIRE

Wildfire is one of the greatest menaces to successful forestry in the South. The region has less than 50 percent of the nation's forest land, but more than 60 percent of its forest fires. In 1957, which firefighters fondly remember as the easiest year in history, the South had "only" 44 thousand forest fires which burned "only" 2.2 million acres, an area considerably larger than the state of Delaware. Between 1956 and 1965, most counties of the Plainsland South, from Louisiana to South Carolina, averaged more than 250 forest fires per million protected acres.[1] The "hot spot" of the South was the "Florida parishes (counties)" of Louisiana and the southern counties of Mississippi, where the norm was more than a thousand fires;

1. M. L. Doolittle, *Forest Fire Occurrence in the South, 1956–1965*, U.S. Forest Service Research Note SO-97 (New Orleans: Southern Forest Experiment Station, 1969).

Livingston Parish, Louisiana (the champion) had 2,454 forest fires per million protected acres for the ten-year period (Fig. 8).

People started 95 percent of the forest fires in the South; foresters have learned to set small fires in order to prevent larger ones. The needles and other debris on the floor of the pine forest are highly flammable, and the forester burns them under controlled conditions before they accumulate to the danger point. Prescribed burning is also an accepted technique for ensuring the natural regeneration of the desired species of pines, which are fire-tolerant, and for eliminating undesirable species.

Farmers in the South have been setting fires for generations in order to clear land for cultivation, or to encourage the growth of new grass and improve grazing by burning off the rank, dead grass of the previous year. Burning the woods was an annual event in the open range and cut-over areas, but "settin' the woods on fire" has been a popular form of outdoor recreation in much of the rural South. On Saturday night, after the boys had had a few snorts, and no one could think of anything better to do, it was always great fun to go out and set the woods on fire. Some Southerners consider firing the woods an established custom that should not be regulated by law. A few set fires because of their intense dislike for the forest service or the paper company that owns the land. Studies by the Forest Service have found that the incidence of forest fires is related fairly closely to low levels of income and education in rural areas.

Attempting to change the woods-burning culture of the South is a very large order, but foresters have used posters and signs, radio and television spots, programs in schools, and Smokey the Bear, in their efforts to educate rural people to the dangers of setting casual fires. The debris-burner does not intend to let his fire get away, but many do, and fires are like fish; the ones that get away are always bigger. Nearly every county in the South has an organized fire protection system. Eminences throughout the region are capped with a detection network of lookout towers, which provide a fine panorama of

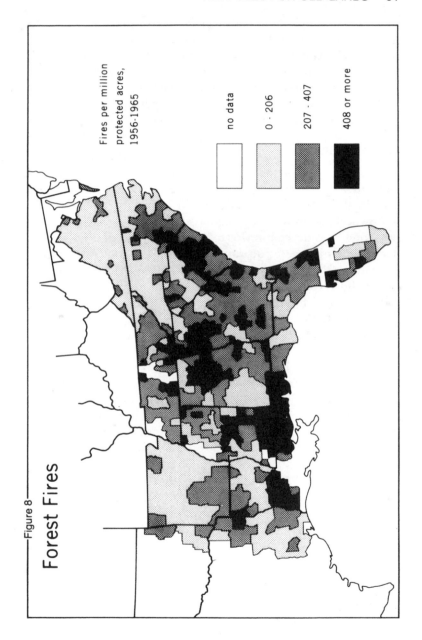

Figure 8

Forest Fires

Fires per million protected acres, 1956-1965

no data

0 - 206

207 - 407

408 or more

the surrounding countryside, as some curious travelers have discovered. Central stations are equipped with hand tools, fire line plows, and tank trucks for the use of fire suppression crews. Often the forest area is criss-crossed with a grid of preplowed fire lines from which to backfire, but the crux of the battle is winning the minds of the people, so that forest fires can be stopped before they ever get started.

PULPWOOD

Although the forests of the old Cotton Belt have produced around a quarter of the nation's lumber since the Second World War, they have produced an even larger share of its pulpwood. Because of its high resin content, southern pine was long considered inferior to northern spruce for the manufacture of bleached pulp and white paper, and it was used primarily for brown kraft paper. Research during the late 1930s, however, showed that southern pine could make good white paper if the trees were cut when they were less than 15 years old, before they developed large quantities of resin. Pulpwood production in the South has increased sixfold since that time.

Between 1952 and 1972 the number of pulpmills in the South increased from 63, with a total daily capacity of 27,000 tons, to 109, with a total daily capacity of 88,000 tons, roughly three-fifths of the national total (Fig. 9). Although the mills are scattered widely through the South, the greatest concentrations are along the Atlantic coast of South Carolina, Georgia, and Florida; around Mobile Bay; and on the sandy lands of Arkansas, Louisiana, and eastern Texas. In 1952 many of the mills were near the coast, but by 1972 there had been considerable expansion into the interior.

Pulpwood is hauled to the mills by truck from a radius of 50 to 60 miles. In addition, most mills have concentration yards up to 200 miles away, where pulpwood is purchased and whence it is brought to the mill by rail. Logs are conveyed from stacks in the mill-woodyard to a large revolving drum for debarking. The clean logs are fed into a chipper and the chips

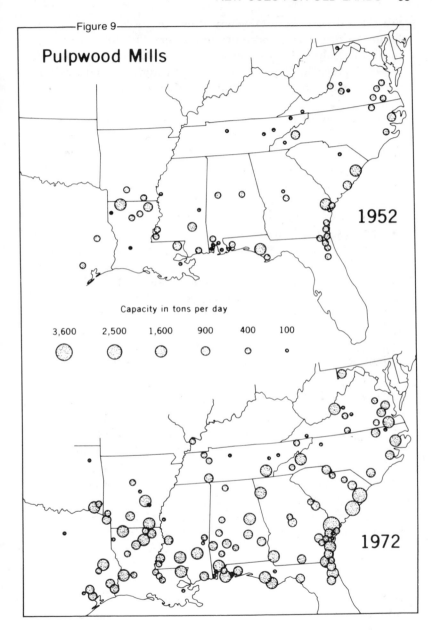

Figure 9

Pulpwood Mills

1952

Capacity in tons per day

3,600   2,500   1,600   900   400   100

1972

are carried to a digester where they are cooked in chemical liquor to dissolve all nonfibrous matter. The brown fibrous mass, or pulp, which comes from the digester is washed, screened, bleached, and then passed through the many rollers and driers of the paper machine to emerge as a sheet of pulp or paper.

An unpleasant by-product of the pulping process is enormous quantities of noxious gases and liquids such as hot-acid sulfite waste. Back in the days before the nation became concerned about environmental pollution, the liquids were merely piped into the nearest river where they killed the fish and made the water unfit for swimming and boating. The gases were released from a stack so tall that they were a bit diluted before they settled on the surrounding area to make eyes burn and skin itch, to peel the paint from houses, and to asphyxiate plants. Every car which left the parking lot next to the mill had to drive through an archway of jet nozzles which sprayed it with clean water to rinse off the acid that had settled upon it in the lot. The abatement of such pollution is very expensive, and the paper industry complained that in 1973 alone it had been compelled to spend roughly half a billion dollars on an activity which it considered essentially nonproductive.

LARGE LANDHOLDINGS

Although a forest of 2,000 to 2,500 acres can provide a comfortable living for a single family, many forest holdings in the old Cotton Belt are much larger than this. Some pulp and paper companies have bought vast acreages of land in order to ensure themselves a dependable supply of raw materials, and several companies hold more than one million acres. The U.S. Forest Service estimated that forest industries in the South owned more than 35 million acres of land in 1970, an area larger than the entire state of Florida, which comprised roughly one-fifth of all the commercial forest land in the region (Fig. 10). The land owned by forest industries is most heavily concentrated in the flatwoods areas of the eastern South and in the sandy lands of Arkansas, Louisiana, Texas,

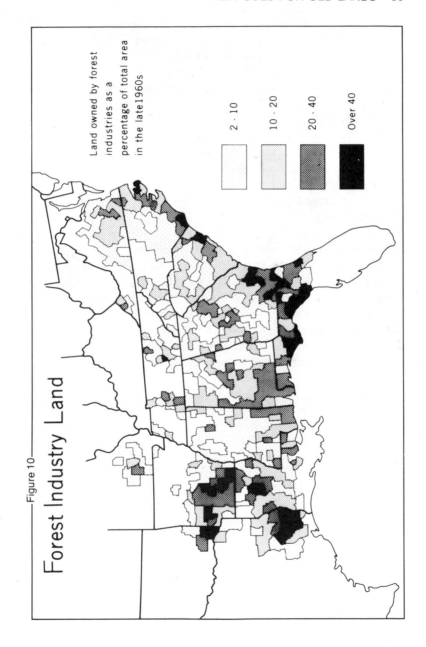

Figure 10

Forest Industry Land

Land owned by forest industries as a percentage of total area in the late 1960s

2 - 10

10 - 20

20 - 40

Over 40

Alabama, and Mississippi. Forest industry companies own 84.5 percent of Dixie County, in Florida's "armpit," and more than 75 percent of nearby Taylor and Franklin counties.

Despite the large amounts of land they own, the forest industry companies still do not have enough to ensure reliable supplies of the raw materials they require, but they have had increasing difficulty in obtaining the additional land they need. There is a host of reasons—land prices have become too high, large tracts seldom come onto the market, owners do not need the money, they are reluctant to part with potentially valuable mineral rights. The forest industries since 1955 have turned more and more from outright purchases to long-term leasing of forest land. By 1970 they held leases on 7 million acres of woodland, an area larger than the entire state of Maryland, in addition to the 35 million acres they owned.

The forest industries set an outstanding example of management for private woodland owners. They employ their own foresters, raise their own seedlings, and engage in extensive reforestation. They maintain their own ranger services and fire-fighting equipment, and cooperate closely with local fire-fighting services. The company forests often are fenced, and some of them are operated as wildlife refuges or private game preserves.

Some private landowners also have large forest holdings which are operated as game preserves. The owners are wealthy northern industrialists who do not live on the land, but only visit it during the fall and winter to relax and shoot quail, leaving it in the hands of a resident manager for the rest of the year. Many of the owners also have showplace farms in other parts of the country, such as the Kentucky Bluegrass area.

—NAVAL STORES

Naval stores were one of the first products of southern pine forests. The living cells of longleaf and slash pines produce a resinous sap or gum, whose flow is greatly stimulated by damage to the trees. In the early days this tarlike gum was used to caulk the seams of wooden vessels and to preserve their ropes and rigging. Turpentine and rosin, its two principal constituents, have been called "naval stores" ever since, despite the fact that they have hundreds of other uses in the modern world. Early production earned North Carolina the nickname of "The Tarheel State," but since 1900 the principal producing district has been in southeastern Georgia and northern Florida, which accounts for about two-thirds of the total world supply.

Gum collection begins in March, when the sap starts to flow. The worker carefully shaves off a strip of bark near the base of the tree and about a third of the way around it. He then nails a spiral collecting gutter across the bottom of the shaved area, and a 2-quart collecting cup at the end of the gutter. After he has "cupped" the tree, he chops off a three-quarter-inch streak of bark above the shaved area, and sprays a sulfuric acid solution along the line where the bark meets the wood at the top of the streak. The acid increases and prolongs the flow of gum, and trees have to be chipped only once every 2 weeks, instead of weekly as in the old days.

The bare working face rises higher and higher along the trunk of the tree as new streaks are chipped every 2 weeks from March until November. The life of a face is 5 or 6 years and then the process is repeated on the opposite side of the tree, leaving a 4-inch bark bar between the two faces as a "life line" through which the tree can receive moisture and minerals from the soil. The crude gum which oozes down into the collecting cups is gathered every 4 to 6 weeks and carried to a turpentine still where it is refined and prepared for shipment to market.

The production of naval stores and pulpwood or sawtimber are competitive activities, because chipping a tree for naval stores retards its growth. The forest manager who wishes to produce both sawtimber and naval stores practices a system of selective cupping. He marks the poorer trees to be cupped and leaves those of better quality to grow to sawtimber size. The tree selected for naval stores production is felled and sold as soon as the faces are finished, for it is unlikely to make worthwhile additional growth. Furthermore, the sawmill operator will pay a lower price for the log, for he knows that his saws may be damaged by nails which have been left in the wood.

DRAINING AND CLEARING

The overall regional trend toward more forest land has been reversed in a few parts of the Plainsland South where wooded areas have been drained, cleared, and brought into cultivation. Many of these areas were so poorly drained that they were not suitable for cotton production, but they can grow fine crops of soybeans. They have been drained and cleared by heavy equipment that has been developed mostly since World War II. Powerful draglines dig deep drainage ditches to carry away the surplus water. Huge bulldozers smash down trees and pile them in windrows for burning, or push them into ditches to be buried. Drainage and clearance on the grand scale have created farm units large enough to make efficient use of the most modern farm machinery available.

A story in the *New York Times* on May 8, 1974, reported that a wealthy trucking magnate, native of North Carolina, had paid an estimated $58 million for 380,000 acres of swampland south of Albemarle Sound in the eastern part of the state, and was draining and clearing it at a cost of $300 an acre. The land will require very careful management after it has been drained, because the rich black peat soil will burn cheerfully if it should happen to catch fire, and subsidence might become a serious problem, but the owner expected to produce bumper crops of corn, and he planned to double-crop soybeans and winter wheat. Pastures were to be developed for thousands of beef cattle, which would be fattened on the corn, and plans were afoot for producing a million hogs a year in 10,000-hog structures which will cost $1 million each. These plans may not come to fruition but the potential of the area is indicated by the fact that a Japanese company had purchased 7,500 acres of land just to the north, and an Italian company had bought 45,000 acres a few score miles to the south.

The largest acreage of land which has actually been drained, cleared, and brought into production since World War II is on the rich alluvial bottomlands of the Delta (Fig. 6). More than 3.5 million acres of fine hardwood forest have been converted to farmland in eastern Arkansas and adjacent states. Perhaps a third of the timber was harvested and sold, but the rest was simply destroyed because farmers were unaware of its value. Soybeans and rice are the most important crops on the new farm land which is not suitable for cotton.

Rice has been a major crop on the Grand Prairie of eastern Arkansas since the early 1900s, and production has expanded onto newly cleared land in the northeastern part of the state since World War II (Fig. 4). Rice farming in Arkansas is highly mechanized. Airplanes seed the crop in flooded fields, and the plants are kept in shallow water until a couple of weeks before they are harvested by giant self-propelled combines. Other large machines are used to dig irrigation canals and drainage ditches, and to construct the low levees which maintain a uniform depth of water in the fields. Most farmers rotate rice with soybeans, but a few have experimented with a rotation of rice and reservoirs which store irrigation water and can also be used to produce buffalo, bass, and catfish. A year or two of rice production is followed by a year or two of fish production on the same field.

GOOBER PEAS

After the boll weevil put them out of the cotton business, some farmers in the old Cotton Belt began to look around for a new money crop. One of the most successful was peanuts, which had originally been imported from Africa on slave ships. Before the Civil War peanuts were grown fairly widely in the South for hog feed, hay, and human munching. Yankee soldiers acquired a taste for these goober peas during the Virginia campaigns, and they took it with them when they returned home after the War. Peanut production expanded in southeastern Virginia and northeastern North Carolina to meet the new national demand. The Virginia-Carolina district remained the principal area of peanut production until World War I, when farmers in southwestern Georgia and southeastern Alabama began to grow peanuts because the boll weevil had wiped out their cotton crops. Peanuts were an important source of vegetable oil during both world wars. In the August, 1942, issue of *The Florida Grower*, J. F. Cooper boasted that "the oil from 12,000 pounds of peanuts will make enough nitroglycerine to fire a 16-inch gun on a battleship. . . . Every time the big gun goes 'boom' the production of nearly 17 acres of Florida peanuts may have been used."

Although peanuts are grown to some extent in many parts of the region, commercial production has become concentrated in two areas (Fig. 4). About half of the national crop is grown in the gently rolling country of southeastern Alabama, southwestern Georgia, and northern Florida. The other important peanut district, in southeastern Virginia and northeastern North Carolina, produces another fifth.

Peanuts usually are grown in rotation with a heavily fertilized crop, such as corn, cotton, or tobacco, for the peanut plant makes efficient use of residual fertility in the soil. After harvest the land is left bare and exposed to the full dangers of water and wind erosion unless a cover crop is planted immediately. The peanut fields at harvest time used to be picturesque, because the plants were cured in stacks before the nuts were removed from the vines. The slender stacks, taller than a man and no more than 3 feet thick, stood in the fields like sentinels for a month to 6 weeks before the nuts were picked and sacked for market; the vines, if properly cured, made good legume hay.

Peanut harvesting has been mechanized in recent years. Machines dig, shake, and windrow the vines, and the crop is combined after it has been cured by a few sunny days. Most of the peanuts produced in the Virginia-Carolina area are salted, but a good part of the Georgia-Alabama crop is made into peanut butter, candy, and vegetable oil. The average American consumes 7 pounds of peanuts and peanut products each year.

Some farmers plant peanuts in alternating rows with corn

and other crops, and turn fattening hogs into the field to harvest it when it is ripe. The peanut growing areas of the South are also the principal hog raising areas.

PASTURES AND CATTLE

The major innovation on former cotton lands which has received the most publicity, far more than forestry or new crops, has been the establishment of pastures and an increase in the number of cattle. Between 1930 and 1960, for example, the acreage of hay land and cleared pasture land, and the number of cattle and calves, increased two-fold in six states of the old Cotton Belt, although even in 1960 these states had less than one acre of every nine in pasture or meadow land.

Many factors contributed to the growing interest in pastures and cattle. Perhaps it started in the Black Belt of Alabama, where much former cotton land had been forced into idleness when the boll weevil hit in 1914. Native grasses began to colonize the abandoned cotton fields, and they were grazed in desultory fashion by livestock, but in the early years little thought was given to good livestock and forage crop management. In fact, the first experimenters who actually put fertilizer on grass were considered ill-informed, until it started to pay off in beef dollars.

The combination of high beef prices and labor shortages during the Second World War stimulated widespread interest in the possibilities of raising cattle. Local champions noted that some of the plants which had been used to control erosion on old cotton fields could provide good forage, and that winters were so mild that cattle could graze out of doors the year round, thus saving the expense of winter feeding and shelter.

Furthermore, cattle farming had a great appeal for successful city business and professional men. The prestige value of land ownership has been strong in the old Cotton Belt ever since plantation days, and the cattle farm provided both tax relief and visible status symbols for the city man. He could invest his money profitably, yet still claim heavy losses for tax purposes by using such devices as licensing his station wagon as a farm vehicle and reporting his chauffeur as a farm worker, to cite two of the most obvious examples.

The cattle farm was a pleasant place to invite friends for the weekend, and it conferred upon its owner a special distinction, the privilege of wearing cowboy regalia. No insignia distinguish the cotton planter, the hog farmer, the forester, the businessman, or the industrialist, but the man who owns a cattle farm is entitled to wear the ten-gallon hat, high-heeled boots, western shirt, and longhorn tie clasp, which make him the envy of his colleagues and all small boys.

The society pages of some newspapers became almost indistinguishable from the farm pages, as bovine matrons posed contentedly with their four-legged friends. Unlike commercial farmers, who made their living from farming, many of the city farmers went in for pure-bred registered livestock. They were a powerful force for improvement, for they could afford to experiment with each new idea that came along. They have had a catalytic effect on the cattle industry in the old Cotton Belt by providing it with a superb field trial laboratory.

THE NEW CATTLE INDUSTRY

In the long run, the health of the cattle industry in the old Cotton Belt depends on the success of commercial farmers, whose sole income is derived from cattle. On farm after farm the owner proudly points to cattle grazing on wide new pastures where once sharecroppers toiled in the hot cotton fields. The old cropper houses are now used as hay barns, and the land which supported a cropper family now carries 5 to 15 cattle. Despite the success of a few cattle farmers, however, the glowing optimism of the early 1950s has been somewhat tempered by experience, and the myth that the South would become a major livestock raising area has never become a reality.[2] The signs that boast that Wilkes County, Georgia, is

2. Merle C. Prunty, "Some Contemporary Myths and Challenges in Southern Rural Land Utilization," *Southeastern Geographer*, Vol. 10, No. 2 (November, 1970), pp. 1–12.

"The County That's Gone to Grass" are still there, but they have become rather weatherbeaten.

Pasture and grazing land in the South has a remarkable range in quality, but most of it is near the bottom end of the scale, and pasture improvement has been scanted because most farms are too small and most farmers lack adequate capital.[3] A successful beef operation requires a minimum of about 100 cattle and 300 acres of good grazing land, but few farms in the old Cotton Belt are large enough to support such an operation, and one has to look very closely at the census dot maps of numbers of cattle and calves, or value of cattle and calves sold, to find any significant concentrations. An enthusiast might identify such areas as the Blackland Prairies of Texas, central Mississippi, or the Black Belt of Mississippi and Alabama, but the South has failed to develop into even a minor beef producing area. Dairy farming might have been successful on smaller farms than are needed for beef, but its growth has been severely handicapped by the lack of any sizable market for dairy products in the South; the only dairy districts are small milksheds which serve major metropolitan areas nearby.

Perhaps the most successful livestock operations have been in piney woods areas where foresters have kept cattle primarily as a fire prevention measure; the animals eat grass which would otherwise accumulate as fuel on the forest floor. Although the native wiregrass provides exceedingly poor forage, and up to 50 acres were needed to carry a single cow, the scrawny piney woods cows were good rustlers, but they did not bring in much money. Some of the cattle were so wild that they could only be rounded up with a .22 rifle. In recent years they have been replaced by better animals as the quality of the pastures has been improved.

The cattle business in the old Cotton Belt has encountered many problems. The old cotton fields had to be fenced, and good fences cost $1,000 or more per mile. Abundant water

3. James R. Anderson, *A Geography of Agriculture in the United States' Southeast*, Geography of World Agriculture, 2 (Budapest: Akademiai Kiado, 1973), p. 63.

had to be provided in the new pastures, because mature beef animals need about 10 gallons a day. The pastures had to be stocked, and some of the neophytes learned to their sorrow that they were not the world's best judges of cattle quality.

Farmers who lacked adequate capital discovered that the agricultural credit system of the South was keyed to cotton, which produced a return in 6 months or so, and they had difficulty in obtaining the longer term loans necessary for a livestock operation. Marketing facilities for cattle had to be developed; initially they were so poor that at least one Georgia cattleman trucked his animals all the way to St. Louis to obtain what he considered a proper price for them.

Some of the more interesting problems revolved around the matter of pasture development, for the region lacks good native forage plants which could provide year-round grazing. This led to experimentation with a variety of hay and pasture crops. The list, which would baffle a botanist, includes at least 11 different kinds of clover (black medic, bur, button, crimson, hop, ladino, lappacea, melilotus, Persian, red, and white), 9 kinds of grasses (Bahia, Bermuda, carpet, Dallis, fescue, Johnson, orchard, rye, and Sudan), 4 kinds of lespedeza (common, Kobe, Korean, and sericea), and 2 kinds of peas (Austrian winter and Caley), not to mention alfalfa, blue lupine, hairy vetch, kudzu, millet, oats, sorghum, and wheat.

Pests became crops, and crops became pests. Farmers who had spent a lifetime battling Johnson grass in their cotton fields suddenly found themselves nursing it tenderly as a hay crop; the Mississippi Agricultural Experiment Station has actually published Information Sheets which tell farmers how to fertilize Johnson grass, or how to eradicate it. Kudzu, an import from Japan, was hailed thusly by an early enthusiast: "one of the best plants known to control erosion . . . increases the fertility of the soil rapidly . . . hay equal in feeding value to alfalfa . . . excellent temporary grazing crop." Kudzu does spread rapidly, by runners which grow as much as 30 feet a year and put down new roots wherever their nodes contact the soil. It so threatened to take over the countryside, in fact, that the Southeastern Forest Experiment Station published a bulletin explaining how to control it.[4]

POULTRY

Although poultry has received less publicity than cattle, poultry numbers have increased phenomenally in certain parts of the old Cotton Belt since the Second World War. In 1949, for example, poultry farmers in Mississippi, Alabama, Georgia, and North Carolina sold approximately 75 million chickens. In 1959 the farmers in these four states sold almost 600 million chickens and had increased their share of national production from 13 percent to 37 percent. In that year the South contained the 18 leading chicken-producing counties in the United States, and 34 of the top 40.

Poultry production in the South is a highly specialized operation. It is remarkably concentrated in a few areas, which are both inside and outside the old Cotton Belt (Fig. 4). The Delmarva (Delaware-Maryland-Virginia) peninsula is the oldest poultry district and the only one that had any appreciable production before World War II. Poultry production became important in north Georgia and northwestern Arkansas immediately after the war, but most of the other poultry districts in the South date only from the 1950s. Poultry farmers in eastern North Carolina's Duplin County, for instance, sold only 42,000 broilers in 1954, but sold 10,317,000 in 1959.

Duplin County provides a reasonably accurate illustration of the way in which poultry farming gets started in a new area. A local entrepreneur, who had been in the theater business, began casting around for new opportunities in the early 1950s. His wife, who was from north Georgia, suggested the possibility of getting into the poultry business, which he very carefully investigated. Eventually, he decided that it was a good risk and borrowed money from feed, hatchery, and processing compa-

4. The fascinating tale of kudzu is told in John J. Winberry and David M. Jones, "Rise and Decline of the 'Miracle Vine': Kudzu in the Southern Landscape," *Southeastern Geographer*, Vol. 13, No. 2 (November, 1973), pp. 61–70.

nies to enable him to set up a small experimental poultry house. He talked one of his neighbors into setting up another at the same time.

Initially there was considerable doubt that local farmers could ever be interested in poultry, for they were primarily tobacco growers, and it was assumed that they would have little time for anything else. Many of the smaller farmers in the county, however, were very conscious of the necessity of increasing the size of their farm businesses, and poultry offered an alternative to taking an off-farm job. Furthermore, it turned out that much of the poultry work could be done by women and children, so there was not a labor shortage. Finally, the middle 1950s, when Duplin County farmers were beginning to think about going into the poultry business, was the period when the relationship between cigarette smoking and lung cancer was being seriously discussed, and this gave cigarette tobacco growers an additional incentive for branching out in new directions.

Three conditions appear essential for the establishment of a new poultry producing district in the South, and all three existed in Duplin County. The first is farmer interest and of that there was little doubt. The first experimental poultry house in the county had been built in 1954, and by 1956 the county extension agent was getting so many questions about the poultry business that he had to have an additional assistant to do nothing else but answer them. Poultry production commonly has developed in problem farm areas; these areas had large numbers of relatively small farms which had low incomes per farm and per family, often where a previous source of income (eggs in Delmarva, fruit in northwestern Arkansas, cotton in Georgia, Alabama, and Mississippi, tobacco in Duplin County) had failed.[5] The second condition required is financing for the construction of poultry houses; this was made available by the Production Credit Association. The third is

5. Jerry Dennis Lord, "The Growth and Localization of the United States Broiler Chicken Industry," *Southeastern Geographer,* Vol. 11, No. 1 (April, 1971), pp. 29–42.

financing for feed and chicks; this was made available by feed companies. Attempts to develop poultry farming in adjacent sections of North Carolina appear to have failed because at least one of these necessary ingredients was lacking.

Duplin County, like the other poultry districts of the South, is dotted with long, low, one-story broiler houses, many of which have automatic feeding and watering systems. Each house holds 10 to 15 thousand chickens, which can be fattened for market in 8 to 10 weeks. Most farmers try to put through at least four flocks a year. This is essentially a factory operation, for much of the feed is shipped in from other areas, and the farmer contributes little more than his labor, buildings, and equipment. A feed merchant or packing company provides him with baby chicks, feed, vitamins, medicines, and supervision. He is guaranteed a set fee per thousand chickens, and shares the profits, if any.

Some farmers mutter that this system, which is known as vertical integration, is merely a new form of sharecropping, because they are not consulted about any management decisions, and are not allowed to decide when to sell the chickens. On the other hand, the farmer is guaranteed a secure return for his labor, and he is not required to risk any of his own capital in the chicken market, which is notorious for its fluctuations.

Two stories illustrate how important the poultry business has become in those parts of the South where it is established. In 1962 it was rumored that Governor Faubus was going to challenge Senator Fulbright for his Senate seat, and that he was going to campaign on the platform that Fulbright's preoccupation with foreign affairs had caused him to neglect his Arkansas constituents. But Fulbright, it is reported, staved off this threat by stumping the civic club circuit with a speech pointing out the percentage of the Arkansas poultry crop that was exported to the European Common Market.

The other story, which comes from north Georgia and is told with great gusto, concerns the small mountain moonshiner who was hauled before the judge for the umpteenth time. He protested loudly, when he was handed a stiff fine and a jail sentence, that the judge had never treated him this way before. "I know," said the judge, "but now a man can make an honest living in these parts by raising poultry, and so he has no business breaking the law by moonshining any longer."

RECYCLING

Poultry operations have become progressively larger. A modern family-sized poultry farm has at least 10,000 birds, and farms with 100,000 birds or more have become common. Growth has created a major materials handling problem because chickens are efficient manure producers; a bird weighing 4 to 5 pounds produces an average of a quarter pound of manure a day, better than a ton a day for a flock of 10,000 birds.[6]

This material can be composted or incinerated, but composting or incineration is the most expensive way to get rid of it. It is cheaper to deposit the material in lagoons or oxidation ditches and wait for nature to take its course, but neighbors tend to complain about the fragrance of such treatment facilities. Ideally the material should be returned to the land as fertilizer; but it takes a lot of land to handle the material from 100,000 busy chickens, and somebody has to be paid to haul and spread the stuff, in addition to the cost of machinery, gas, and oil.

In recent years scientists have made a major breakthrough in managing manure: recycle it back through the animals. It's a lot cheaper to dry it out and feed it back to the chickens than it is to haul it out and spread it. The first step is baking. Raw material from batteries of laying hens is subjected to temperatures high enough to destroy its pathogens. Out of the drying equipment comes a light-brown odorless material called dried layer waste (DLW to the dainty) which reportedly resembles soybean meal, at least in appearance. The drying equipment

6. R. Gar Forsht, Clark R. Burbee, and William M. Crosswhite, *Recycling Poultry Waste as Feed: Will It Pay?*, Agricultural Economic Report No. 254 (Washington: U. S. Department of Agriculture, Economic Research Service, 1974).

is too expensive for a family-sized operation of only 10,000 birds, but an efficient, modern farm of 50,000 birds or more could depend on DLW for about one-eighth of its total feed requirements if only the U.S. Food and Drug Administration could disabuse itself of some of its quaint prejudices.

DLW might also be used to provide part of the protein requirements of beef and dairy cattle, and they don't seem to notice the difference, at least not after they get used to it. Old-fashioned corn-fed beef could become a thing of the past; perhaps as a next step we need no more than the right kind of packaging and some clever Saturday morning television commercials to sell us on the idea of bypassing animals completely and using DLW for direct human consumption with milk and sugar at breakfast. We might not notice the difference either.

Broiler waste presents a few more problems, because it is a mixture of manure and absorptive litter, such as wood shavings or peanut hulls. It has been ground and used as a not too satisfactory replacement for hay in feeding beef cattle, but if it is stored for two months in an oxygen-free silo it becomes a sweet-smelling, palatable, and apparently pathogen-free roughage with a 25 percent protein content. A farmer who combines beef and broiler operations might increase his income from both by ensiling broiler waste and feeding it to his beef cattle. A man with 200 steers and 100,000 broilers might save $6,000 or more a year on the cost of feed for his beef cattle by running his broiler waste through them.

ENVOI

Cotton has ceased to be king of the Plainsland South. Cotton production is still important in a few favored sections of the old Cotton Belt, but large areas which once were dominated by cotton are now producing new specialty crops, pastures and livestock, forest products, or some combination of these and other new commodities. Furthermore, even at the height of his reign, King Cotton never ruled supreme throughout the Plainsland South, for much of the northeastern corner has always been tobacco country.

4 Tobacco Country

The northeastern corner of the Plainsland South differs in two important respects from other parts of the region. In the first place, this has traditionally been tobacco country. Cotton never penetrated very far northward into Virginia, and even in North Carolina it has faced serious competition from tobacco for pride of place as the leading money crop.

Secondly, many sections of Maryland, Delaware, and northern Virginia are really part of the Northeast, rather than the South, despite the fact that they are usually considered part of the South, and even have a few Southern traits. These are the areas which have come under the influence of the great urban complex which sprawls northward from Washington to Boston, a complex which the French geographer Gottmann calls Megalopolis. Megalopolis provides a huge market for all manner of fruits and vegetables grown on the sandy lands around Chesapeake Bay, and it spills its wealth into the countryside in neatly manicured "gentleman farms." The influence of Megalopolis has pulled these areas out of the South.

SOUTHERN MARYLAND

Tobacco was the cornerstone of the economy of the Chesapeake Bay country for almost two centuries before cotton became an important plantation crop in the South. In colonial times each planter had his own tidewater landing where ocean-going ships could tie up for loading. Slaves packed the tobacco in large wooden barrels, called hogsheads, which held 600 to 700 pounds, and rolled the hogsheads down to the wharves.

In order to reduce labor, the wharves were located as far inland and upstream as possible, but unfortunately this also is where danger of siltation was greatest. Tobacco cultivation is unusually conducive to soil erosion, and sediment has filled many former navigation channels, turning open bodies of water into mud flats. Port Tobacco, Maryland, for example, an important seaport in colonial times, is now more than a mile above the head of tidewater.

Five counties in southern Maryland, on the peninsula between Chesapeake Bay and the Potomac River, are the last of the old tobacco producing districts of the Chesapeake Bay country (Fig. 4).[1] Maryland tobacco has thin, light, dry, chaffy leaves of a reddish-brown color. They burn very well, with almost no aroma, and are used in most cigarette blends to ensure good burning. Most American blends contain only 2 to 4 percent Maryland tobacco, but cigarettes containing a very high proportion are in great favor in Switzerland, and much of the crop is exported there.

Southern Maryland has rectangular tobacco barns, usually 30 by 60 feet and 16 feet to the eaves, for curing the green leaf. When the plant is ripe, the farmer chops it off near the ground and spears the butt of the stalk on a lath-like tobacco stick. The sticks, each holding six stalks, are hung in the barn for several months to allow the leaves to dry. This process is known as air curing. The sides of most barns have hinged vertical ventilating doors which can be opened in good weather and closed in bad to hasten the curing process. The leaves are stripped from the stalk when they are cured or dry, and they are tied into bundles called hands.

1. John Fraser Hart and Eugene Cotton Mather, "The Character of Tobacco Barns and Their Role in the Tobacco Economy of the United States," *Annals of the Association of American Geographers*, Vol. 51 (1961), pp. 274–93.

The crop is hauled to a tobacco warehouse in a nearby town and sold at auction. The warehouse is a cavernous one-story building whose roof is crisscrossed with serried rows of sky-lights. For much of the year it is a vast hollow shell, but it comes to life during the brief 6 to 8 week market season. The hands of tobacco are stacked neatly on wicker baskets lined up across the warehouse floor. The sale of each basket begins when the warehouse manager calls out a starting price to the auctioneer and the buyers from tobacco manufacturing com-panies. The auctioneer calls out the bidding in his famous singsong chant as the buyers indicate their bids with furious hand signals. The baskets are sold at a rate of one every 8 to 10 seconds.

BRIGHT TOBACCO

The early settlers who left the Chesapeake Bay country took tobacco seeds with them as they moved westward onto the Piedmont. The original Virginia tobacco plant, which pro-duced a strong, heavy, dark-green leaf, underwent a startling transformation when farmers planted its seeds on some infer-tile light-grey soils of the North Carolina Piedmont. When grown under conditions of semistarvation, the plant produced a mild, thin, light-green leaf. The new leaf proved so popular that tobacco production spread rapidly in North Carolina, while local boosters began boasting about how much poor land their counties had.

Carolina tobacco farmers learned that they could produce an even better leaf by continuing semistarvation into the cur-ing process. The old heavy leaves had been cured by hanging them up to dry, as in modern southern Maryland, or by smok-ing them over open fires. The new process used high tempera-tures for rapid drying, and produced a golden orange-yellow leaf which became known as Bright tobacco. Bright tobacco is also known as flue-cured tobacco, because of the curing process. It is also called Virginia tobacco, despite the fact that the bulk of the crop is grown in North Carolina. Only a very small acreage of the old original heavy leaf is now grown in Virginia.

Although Bright tobacco had been grown as early as the 1840s, its fame was spread widely by an incident which occurred at the end of the Civil War, when General Joseph E. Johnston was surrendering to General W. T. Sherman near Durham's Station, North Carolina. The men of both armies helped themselves to free samples from John Ruffin Green's tobacco factory, and completely looted it. Shortly afterward Green began to receive letters from the widely dispersed soldiers, asking where they might obtain more of his lighter, milder tobacco.

Green had given his tobacco the trade name Bull Durham, a name which was soon made famous by aggressive salesmanship and one of the first comprehensive advertising campaigns in the United States. Although Bright tobacco made an attractive wrapper for plugs of chewing tobacco, most of the crop was used in the manufacture of cigarettes, which did not really become popular until after the First World War. The demand for Bright tobacco has risen in accord with the growing demand for cigarettes; for just over half of a cigarette blend consists of Bright tobacco, and per capita consumption of cigarettes in the United States rose from two a week in 1910, to one a day in 1918, to ten a day in 1958. Tobacco growers became gravely concerned when medical research linked some forms of cancer to smoking, and stringent regulations were placed on the advertising and sale of cigarettes. Yet cigarette consumption in the United States has remained fairly steady at around 200 packs per person, per year.

Bright tobacco production spread at the expense of cotton. Farmers in eastern North Carolina switched to tobacco when cotton prices dropped disastrously during the 1880s, and within a decade tobacco had also become an important crop in parts of eastern South Carolina. During the late 1910s Bright tobacco production spread into southern Georgia and northern Florida in the wake of the boll weevil. Today Bright tobacco is a major crop in much of eastern North Carolina and the adjacent states, and in the south Georgia-north Florida area (Fig. 4).

The government price support program for Bright tobacco was once tied to a system of acreage allotments quite similar to the system used for cotton, but so many farmers emphasized quantity at the expense of quality that the basis of the system was changed from acreage to production. Each tobacco farmer was allotted a poundage quota which specified the number of pounds he was permitted to sell. Poundage quotas could be leased and transferred, but only within a single county. The degree to which government controls can freeze the geography of a crop was illustrated by a study which estimated that quotas for 123 million pounds of tobacco would have been transferred from the western part of North Carolina to the eastern part in 1968 if quotas could have been transferred across county lines, and that quotas for 67 million pounds of tobacco would have been transferred from Virginia and North Carolina to South Carolina and Georgia if quotas could have been transferred across state lines.

The Bright tobacco countryside is dotted with square tobacco barns, some 16 to 20 feet on a side and 20 feet high, which are built of clay-chinked logs, cinderblock, or frame sheathed in green or black tarpaper. Two 12-inch flues (whence the name flue-cured) of sheet-metal piping extend across the barn floor from a square brick furnace on one side. The furnace, fired from the outside by wood, fuel oil, gas, or coal, is protected beneath the shelter of a lean-to roof attached to the side of the barn above it. The furnace is fired after the barn has been filled with tobacco, and the inside temperature is gradually raised to about 170°F. A complete cure, which changes the green leaf to a bright orange-yellow color, normally requires 3½ to 5 days.

The Bright tobacco harvest extends over a period of 6 to 8 weeks. The tobacco field must be picked over about once a week, for each leaf is picked as it becomes ripe. A normal harvest crew may consist of as many as 10 to 12 workers. Stooped-over pickers walk down between the rows, pull 2 to 4 leaves from each plant, and place them in mule-drawn sleds with waist-high burlap sides. A child drives the loaded sled to the barn, where the leaves are tied to a tobacco stick and hung inside for curing. The barn is emptied as soon as the cure is completed, and a new batch of tobacco is hung.

Most operations on a Bright tobacco farm, from seedbed preparation to harvest, require large amounts of labor, and efforts to mechanize production and harvesting have been singularly unsuccessful. The tobacco district of the eastern Carolinas has the densest rural farm population in the entire United States, and Negroes comprise a high percentage of the total. This is one of the few areas in the South where the Negro population has not been decimated by outmigration, and it provides an attractive "fishing pond" for employment agencies in northern cities. The "Help Wanted" columns of local newspapers regularly carry advertisements for domestic jobs in the North at wages higher than are offered white workers in this area.

The Georgia-Florida district is more sparsely populated and the labor problem is correspondingly serious. As one wool-hat farmer near Baxley, Georgia, described it, "First o' the season you round up a gang o' workers for pickin', and they work for you jes' one day a week. Miss a day an' you got to wait a week! Somebody dies when you puttin' in tobacco, why you jes' let him lay there an' keep puttin' it in."

GADSDEN COUNTY

The smallest and most spectacular tobacco district in the Plainsland South is centered in north-central Florida's Gadsden County (Fig. 4). Farmers in this district specialize in producing thin, extra-fine leaves which are used for the outer wrappers of cigars. Their farms have a remarkable complex of five elements: huge tentlike "shades" under which tobacco is grown; subordinate crops of corn and peanuts; clusters of huge barns for curing tobacco and fattening cattle; sumptuous homes; and squalid shacks.

Gadsden County became an important tobacco producing district in the 1890s, after a local farmer imported seed from

Sumatra. Another farmer, on a visit to Cuba, noticed that tobacco grown in the shade of trees produced a thinner leaf of finer texture, and he began to experiment with the use of artificial shade in growing tobacco.

Since 1900 the entire tobacco crop in Gadsden County has been grown under specially constructed shades, vast flat tents of open mesh white or yellow cloth which may cover several acres or more. The cloth is sewn to galvanized wires stretched taut between pine or red cedar posts set in precise 32 foot squares. The shades simulate a moist tropical climate by reducing wind velocity and evaporation, and thus increasing humidity. They also afford some protection from direct sunlight, hail, and insects.

The shades are 9 feet above the ground and their sides can easily be raised to allow workers to enter. Most of the work is done by Negroes with mules, for no machine could go through the rows without bruising the leaves. The leaves are harvested one at a time as they become ripe, and are cured in huge barns 40 by 120 feet, and 20 feet to the eaves. As in southern Maryland, the leaves are air-cured by hanging to dry.

Along the sides of the barns are shutterlike wooden windows which can be swung open for light and air. Both are essential, because the barns are used to fatten cattle after the tobacco crop has been removed. The cattle are used as fertilizer factories to produce the manure which is so much needed to maintain the fertility of the sandy soil. Each barn holds about one hundred cattle, which are fattened in 120 days and produce around 300 tons of manure, or enough for about 20 acres of tobacco land.

The tobacco farmers grow corn for cattle feed, and peanuts whose shells provide litter for the barn floors. In addition, they buy concentrates, cottonseed, citrus pulp, and molasses to feed the cattle. The cattle are fed inside the barns to protect the manure from the severe leaching which would otherwise occur in the humid subtropical climate.

The barns often stand in clusters of five or more, for the heavy capital investment required for shades and barns has concentrated tobacco farming in the hands of corporations or large private operators. The sumptuous homes of the farm owners and managers contrast dramatically with the clusters of 2 to 20 squalid shacks in which their Negro workers live.

EPITOME

Although the South produces most of the nation's tobacco, it produces several different kinds under different conditions which result in quite distinctive geographic landscapes. The crop is grown in the open in southern Maryland, whereas it is grown under unique cheesecloth shades in Gadsden County, Florida. In both these areas the leaf is air-cured in large barns, but in the Bright tobacco country of the Carolinas and Georgia the leaf is flue-cured in smallish, squat, square barns which can be heated to very high temperatures to produce the desired qualities.

5 The Border Hills

The northern part of the South consists of two large upland areas which are almost completely separated from each other (Figs. 5 and 6). In the east the Appalachian Uplands stretch from Pennsylvania to northern Alabama. They occupy most of West Virginia, Kentucky, and Tennessee, and spill over into smaller portions of adjacent states. The Appalachian Uplands are connected with the Ozark Uplands of Missouri and Arkansas by the Shawnee Hills of southern Illinois. These two upland areas have remarkably complex patterns of land use, for they have some of the finest farm land in the United States and some of the very poorest, often in close proximity.

The Border Hills have three broad types of land (Fig. 6). Areas of Appalachian Land Type are hilly to mountainous, with shallow stony soils of low productivity (Fig. 5). The mountainous sections have deep valleys, steep slopes, and narrow ridges. Cleared areas are concentrated on the slender strips of alluvial bottomland along the major streams, but most of the land is covered with deciduous hardwood forests dominated by oak, maple, hickory, and yellow poplar, or tuliptree (Fig. 7). The hilly sections have larger acreages of crop and pasture land (Figs. 12 and 13), but most of the hill land is also wooded.

At the other extreme, areas of Midcontinent Land Type

have relatively gentle topography and productive soils which support prosperous farming, and woodland is fairly scarce. The largest concentrations of cropland in the South are in areas of Midcontinent and Delta Land Type (Fig. 12). Areas of Ozark Border Land Type have a complex mixture of poor hilly districts interspersed with fairly extensive areas of good to moderately productive soil. As a general rule, the better areas are used for cropland and pasture, and the rougher areas are wooded, but the use of the land is often determined by the whims and capabilities of individual farmers rather than by its inherent quality.

The nature of the land surface and the quality of the soil are related fairly intimately to the kind of rock which lies beneath them. Sandstone, as a general rule, gives rise to rough country, often with spectacular cliffs, and coarse sandy soils which are deficient in plant nutrients. Shale, on the other hand, commonly underlies lowland areas with poorly drained clay soils which are not highly productive. Limestone is also associated with lowlands, but more frequently with loamy soils which are well supplied with plant nutrients and are generally productive if they are properly managed.

EARLY SETTLERS

The Border Hills were settled in the first great westward push of the American frontier. Pioneers had occupied most of the coves and valleys of the Appalachian Uplands by 1810, and the Ozark Uplands were occupied during the next generation, at a time when Chicago was still only a struggling outpost in the wilderness. After the initial surge, however, almost no new settlers moved into these areas, and for almost a century time simply passed them by.

Many of the early settlers were hardy Ulster Scots, descendants of Scots who had been settled in the ancient Irish province of Ulster more than a century before they had moved to the New World. The fiercely independent Ulster Scot was one of the great frontiersmen of America. He was as lean, tough, and self-reliant as the Indian, and needed only his axe and rifle, powder and lead, knife and tomahawk, to subsist happily in the wilderness. Fearing God alone, and distrusting all other authority, he felt crowded when another settler built his cabin only a couple of miles away. He strapped his meager belongings on the back of his horse and plodded off with his family to seek a better place to live.

Some of the best routes through the mountains followed the level crests of the ridges. The pioneers discovered that nearly every ridge had a "bear trail."[1] A short strenuous climb was necessary to reach the crest, but the land on top was fairly level, the underbrush was less dense, no rivers had to be crossed, there were no rattlesnakes or copperheads, and it was easier to spot Indians or wild animals. Before long the settlers began using the level ridgetops, or balds, as summer grazing areas for their cattle, just as their forebears in Scotland and Ireland had taken their livestock to the hill grazings in summer. Cattle were rarely attacked by bears, panthers, or wolves, but the settlers did not dare graze other livestock on the balds until these predators had been eliminated. The steep hill slopes served as natural fences which kept the cattle away from the crops on fields along the valley bottomlands, and saved the labor of constructing split rail fences.

MOUNTAIN FEUDS

The Civil War brought bitter days to the mountains of West Virginia and Kentucky, which lay in the border zone between North and South. Neighbor was turned against neighbor, and even families were divided. Regular forces fought back and forth across the area, but the mountain people also suffered from the depredations of lawless bands of ruffians who roamed the countryside robbing, murdering, plundering, and destroying. Cabins were burned, men were ambushed, and husbands were slain before the very eyes of their wives and children.

The bitter hatreds engendered by the war became the ferocious mountain feuds which lingered on for half a century or

1. Phil Gersmehl, "Factors Leading to Mountaintop Grazing in the Southern Appalachians," *Southeastern Geographer*, Vol. 10, No. 1 (April, 1970), pp. 67–72.

so. Widows swore their children to avenge the deaths of their murdered fathers, and families learned to hate each other's very names long after the original cause for hatred had been forgotten. The feud between the Hatfields of Logan County, West Virginia, and the McCoys of Pike County, Kentucky, was the most famous, but every mountain county had its own bloody feud, and many had more than one.

Some of the mountain feuds carried over into politics, where the battle between Yankee and Rebel became the fight between Republicans and Democrats. Many mountain counties have remained staunch in their allegiance to one party or the other ever since the Civil War. Some of the "mountain Republican" counties have been even more loyal to their party than many Democratic counties in the Solid South (Figs. 18 and 19).

MOUNTAIN MOONSHINE

The whiskey still was almost as much a part of traditional mountain life as the rifle and the spinning wheel. The Ulster Scots had brought knowledge of distilling with them from Ireland, and they began to make whiskey almost as soon as they had harvested their first crop of corn. Whiskey provided a brief release from the hardships and monotony of their lives, and it also provided a convenient way to sell their corn, which was too heavy to carry to market unless it was converted into a beverage of high value.

Many mountain people have seen nothing wrong in making and selling corn whiskey, and they have resented those who taxed them for doing so. The battle between moonshiner and revenue officer reached its peak during Prohibition days. Revenue agents combed the hills, county sheriffs deputized a small army of agents to help them, and in many mountain counties an average of a still a day was discovered and destroyed. The moonshiners concealed their stills with great skill and cunning, and posted lookouts to warn them of approaching agents. When the lawmen made their final rush on a still they never knew whether they could expect to find a deserted site, capture the moonshiners, or have to fight a pitched battle with them. In one single mountain county 16 deputies were shot to death in a 4-year period during Prohibition.

Moonshining did not die with the demise of Prohibition, but it has changed somewhat. In the summer of 1965 a captured still adorned the sheriff's office in McCreary County, Kentucky, but the sheriff said that many of the smaller operators who produced mainly for family consumption had gone out of business because they didn't like having to face a Federal judge. Modern mountain moonshiners, who may produce as much as 20 million gallons of illegal whiskey a year, are commercial operators who work on a fairly large scale. Most of them produce a vile product which nonetheless commands a good market because of high taxes on legal liquors, and because local option keeps many mountain counties legally "dry."

MOUNTAIN FARMERS

The early settler and his family made or grew almost everything they needed. He cleared a small patch of land and built a rude cabin of logs. His wife and children tended the food crops of corn, beans, and squash. He made some of the corn into whiskey and grew a little tobacco. Cotton and flax were grown for fibers which his wife could make into homespun clothing.

The pioneer kept a few hound dogs to warn him against surprise by Indians or approaching visitors, and to help him hunt the wild game which provided meat for his table. When game became scarce, he started turning loose hogs and cattle to forage for themselves in the woods. To get what little money he needed he sold skins, surplus tobacco or whiskey, or perhaps cut down a few trees and floated them downstream to a sawmill.

Many mountain farmers have continued to lead a semi-subsistence life until very recently. Every family had its milk cow, hogs, chickens, vegetable garden, and orchard. Most of the better valley land was used for corn, hay, or pasture, with tiny patches of tobacco as a money crop. The sole cash income of some mountain farmers has been derived from less than an acre of tobacco.

Farm income in the mountains is painfully meager, and levels of living are low; the mountains of eastern Kentucky are one of the deepest pockets of poverty in the entire United States (Fig. 1). Many mountain farms are fairly large in total acreage, but they are still too small to provide a decent living because so much of the land cannot be cultivated. They cannot be enlarged effectively because most of the good level land is strung along the creek bottoms in narrow strips. And even if they could be enlarged several times, many mountain farms would still be too small for efficient use of modern methods and machinery.

The mountain farm which could support the primitive existence of a century or even a generation ago can no longer provide an adequate living for a modern family, for the children aspire to higher living standards than their parents have enjoyed. As one mountain farmer said, "The tractor has replaced the mule, and it eats cash instead of corn." And a knowledgeable county agent commented, "You just can't live on a 10-acre farm any more. The family cow and the hog have gone out, and so has the orchard, and almost the garden too. The farmer now buys everything from the grocery store just as you and I do."

Many of the young people have departed, and the population declined steadily at each census between 1940 and 1970 in the mountain counties of Kentucky and West Virginia (Fig. 2), but in 1970 these counties still had a remarkably dense rural population because of their high birth rates (Fig. 15). The Ozarks were settled later than Appalachia, and their population was never nearly so dense, but some Ozark counties also lost population steadily between 1940 and 1970.

LAND ABANDONMENT

The mountainous sections of West Virginia and Kentucky have some of the poorest and most intractable land in the eastern half of the United States. Between 1945 and 1960 approximately 3 million acres of cleared farm land were abandoned in Kentucky, and 2 million more were abandoned in West Virginia. The rate of abandonment was greatest in the rugged, isolated, and inaccessible areas of eastern Kentucky and southern West Virginia, where 2 of every 3 acres of cleared farm land in 1910 had been abandoned by 1960. Many entire farms at "the head of the hollow" have been abandoned because they do not have adequate roads, schools, electricity, telephones, and other appurtenances of modern life.

Some mountain land is simply not worth the cost of equipment, fencing, livestock, lime, fertilizer, seed, and especially, labor, to maintain it in agricultural production. The man who has the necessary capital to invest in such land would be much better advised to buy a good farm elsewhere rather than to try to upgrade a poor one in the mountains. This is part of a national pattern; to an increasing degree agricultural labor and capital are both becoming concentrated on the better land in the United States, and the poorer land is being abandoned.

Some poor land in the mountains is still being farmed, however, because it happens to be near a highway, whereas better but less accessible land has been abandoned. On the other hand, automobiles and improved highways have made off-farm jobs more widely available, and today many former farm families live on the farm and obtain their income from nonfarm sources. The head of the family may continue to fiddle around with a little part-time farming, or he may be too tired after a hard day's work and a long drive home.

The decision as to whether or not farm land will be abandoned may also be a function of age. An energetic young man may farm poor land because it is the best he has, whereas an older man who owns better land may not farm it at all. Many older farmers are eking out a meager subsistence with the aid of such government payments as welfare, Social Security, Soil Bank, and the like. In Whitley County, Kentucky, for instance, the total value of all farm products sold in 1959 was $1,142,000. In 1964 some 4,479 of the county's 25,815 people received Social Security payments totalling $2,460,000; 854 people received old-age assistance totalling $542,000; 378 families received $435,000 in aid to dependent children; 143 disabled people received $110,000; and 56 blind people received $40,000. In addition, the Social Security district office here had 30 employees with a payroll of $175,000, and the district office of the Department of Economic Security had 11 employees and a payroll of $45,000.

LAND CLEARANCE

Although land abandonment is fairly widespread in the more rugged and intractable sections of the Border Hills, in many of the intermediate areas where farming is not so difficult, one can today observe the paradox of some land being abandoned and some land being cleared, often on neighboring farms and sometimes even on the same farm.[2] Simultaneous abandonment and clearance is a continuation of a traditional system of "brush fallow" which seems to have been common throughout the hills of Appalachia from the very earliest days of settlement. The farmer grew corn and tobacco until the soil washed away, or became too severely eroded for further cultivation. He then forgot about the land, or abandoned it to pasture. If this pasture land were not mowed at least once a year it would grow up in weeds, blackberry briers, sassafras and sumac bushes, and persimmon sprouts. Eventually it reverted to poor quality, second growth woodland. As other land on the farm wore out, this growth of brush and woodland might be cleared once again.

Land clearance has become increasingly important in recent years for two reasons. First, a small farmer with a limited acreage of land can hardly afford to allow any of it to lie fallow. The possibility of converting unused brushland into an additional source of farm income holds tremendous appeal. Sec-

2. John Fraser Hart, "Abandonment of Farm Land in Kentucky," *Southeastern Geographer*, Vol. 4 (1964), pp. 1–10.

ond, the chore of clearance has been greatly simplified by new machines such as the bulldozer and brush hog, which can uproot and clear away fairly good sized brush, and the bog disc, which can ride over obstacles and level the land. After the land has been cleared and levelled, it must be limed, fertilized, and seeded to turn it into pasture.

Many of the newly cleared pastures have a pathetically low carrying capacity, ranging from 3 to 10 acres and up per mature animal unit. For the most part, they are used to graze dairy cattle of inferior quality. Yields are low and most of the milk goes to creameries rather than into the more lucrative fluid milk market. Despite the low return they produce, the small dairy herds (which rarely exceed 20 milking cows) have enabled many small farmers to hang on to a meager subsistence by applying their labor to a combination of dairying and tobacco farming, while their womenfolk commute to low-paying jobs in the nearest factory. One farmer in eastern Kentucky told me that he was "a real mountain go-getter; I got my wife a job at the pajama plant, and every day at five I go get her."

It would appear that land clearance, in many instances, is merely postponing the inevitable. In the past many farmers in the hills of Appalachia have derived much of their cash income from a small patch of tobacco, which rarely has run as large as an acre. The addition of a tiny dairy herd can easily double the gross farm cash income, but income still remains pitifully small. In a sense, land clearance has converted semisubsistence tobacco farms into semisubsistence tobacco-dairy farms. Although these farms might provide an acceptable standard of living for some members of the older generation, they will hold little attraction for most young people.

MINING AREAS

Mining is an important activity in a number of areas in the Border Hills (Fig. 11). The Index of Mining Employment, a sophisticated measure of the importance of mining in each county, is based on the assumption that mining is not important in a county where the percentage of the labor force em-

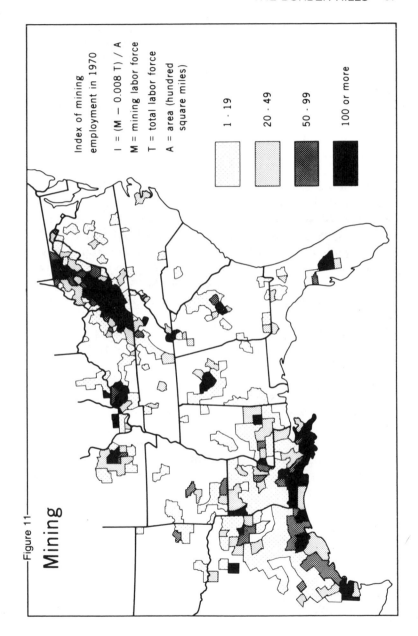

Figure 11

Mining

Index of mining employment in 1970

$I = (M - 0.008\,T) / A$

M = mining labor force

T = total labor force

A = area (hundred square miles)

1 - 19

20 - 49

50 - 99

100 or more

ployed in mining is below the national level.[3] Eight-tenths of one percent of the labor force of the United States was employed in mining in 1970, so a county is not considered a mining county if less than 0.8 percent of its labor force was employed in mining in that year.

The first step in calculating the Index of Mining Employment for any county in 1970 is to multiply the total number of persons in the labor force (T) by eight-tenths of one percent (0.008). The result is subtracted from the number of persons employed in mining (M), and divided by the area of the county (A) to compensate for variations in county size. The resulting value for each county is multiplied by 100 so that all index numbers are whole numbers. As an example, in 1970 Mineral County, West Virginia, had an area (A) of 330 square miles and a total labor force (T) of 7,375 workers, of whom 92 were employed in mining (M). Multiplying T (7,375) by 0.008 gives a value of 59, which is subtracted from M (92), and the result (33) is divided by A (330) for a value of 0.10, or an Index of Mining Employment of 10.

Mining areas are scattered through the Border Hills (Fig. 11). Frenchmen were mining lead on the eastern flank of the St. Francois dome in eastern Missouri as early as 1720. Most of the shallow mines in the old lead belt have been closed, but during the 1960s deeper mines were opened in the new lead belt, which runs through Viburnum on the western flank of the dome.

Copper is mined at Copperhill in the southeastern corner of Tennessee. Sulfur fumes from early smelting operations denuded the surrounding countryside, turning a wooded area into a manmade desert. This area is one of the wettest parts of the eastern United States, with more than sixty inches of precipitation a year, and heavy rains pelting the bare ground have created a veritable museum of the effects of erosion in a perhumid climate.

3. John Fraser Hart, "A Map of Mining Employment in the United States in 1960," *Minnesota Geographer*, Vol. 22, No. 2 (April, 1970), pp. 1–8.

Bituminous coal is the most important mineral of the Border Hills. One major producing district is the Western Coal Field of Kentucky and adjacent parts of Illinois and Indiana. Another is the Warrior Basin at the southern end of the Appalachian coal field in north central Alabama. The most important, of course, is the great coal field of eastern Kentucky and southern West Virginia.

COAL COUNTRY

One of the world's largest coal deposits lies hidden beneath the hills and mountains of Appalachia. The coal fields of eastern Kentucky and southern West Virginia produce approximately one-third of all the bituminous coal mined in the United States. Large-scale coal mining did not begin here until fairly late, around 1910, when railroads were first driven into the hills. The mining companies brought in a few supervisory technicians, but most of the pick and shovel work was done by mountain people who flocked into the booming mining camps.

For a decade or so the coal fields were prosperous, and production expanded rapidly during the First World War. Then coal prices slumped during the late 1920s, which led to bitter troubles between management and labor. In May, 1931, fifty miners and ten deputy sheriffs fought a pitched battle near Evarts, Kentucky, in which two deputies and one miner were killed. Slayings which occurred during the efforts of the United Mine Workers to organize the mines gave Harlan County, Kentucky, its nickname of Bloody Harlan, although it had no more trouble than half a dozen other coal field counties.

Coal mining recovered considerably during the Second World War, as demands for coal increased, but the old pick and shovel methods of underground mining have changed enormously. Most of the men in the mines have been replaced by continuous mining machines, whose steel claws tear coal from the seam, scoop it up, and load it onto endless conveyor belts in a single integrated operation. Four to six men with a continuous mining machine can produce twice as much coal per day as 60 men with picks and shovels.

A great deal of coal mining has now come above the surface, where coal is mined by a technique known as stripping.[4] The strip miner uses a giant power shovel to tear away the soil and rock, or overburden, which covers the coal seam. This "spoil," which is dumped to one side, is so heavy and sour that nothing will grow on it unless it is heavily limed and fertilized.

In level to rolling areas the strip miner makes a box cut, with a spoil bank on one side, and a highwall of undisturbed rock on the other. Smaller shovels dig out the coal which is exposed at the bottom of the cut, and load it onto trucks to be hauled away. After the coal has been removed, the power shovel makes a second box cut parallel to the first, and dumps the spoil into the first cut. Over time the operation produces a badland of unsightly razorback ridges. The final cut often contains orange or rust colored water made strongly acid by contact with the organic matter of the coal seam.

In rougher areas the strip miner makes a bench cut which snakes around the hills and mountains, following the contours. The highwall is on the inside of the bench; the spoil is shoved over the edge and goes crashing down the slope, smashing trees, crumpling houses, burying fields and pastures, blocking roads, and damming streams. The steep unstable spoil banks pose a constant threat of landslides. Strip mines have gashed more than 20,000 miles of raw unsightly benches into the hillsides of Appalachia.

Normally a strip mine operation cannot profitably remove more than about 10 feet of overburden for each foot of coal seam thickness. Many mines cannot penetrate very far into the mountainside because of the depth of overburden. Areas such as this call for a new machine known as a coal auger. The coal auger is a giant diesel-driven screw which bores into the face of a coal seam and brings out a continuous stream of coal. The

4. *Surface Mining and Our Environment: A Special Report to the Nation* (Washington, D.C.: U.S. Department of the Interior, 1967).

largest augers, which are operated by a single person seated at an electric control panel, can bore as far as a thousand feet into the earth.

Despite the hideous scars it leaves, strip mining has increased rapidly since World War II because it is cheaper and safer, has a higher output per man, and recovers a higher percentage of coal than underground mining. As Americans began to become more concerned about the quality of the environment, however, strip mining came under increasingly heavy attack, and in 1974 Congress passed a bill which would have required strip mine operators to restore the land to its original contours and use. Coal mining and electric power companies violently opposed this bill, and circulated alarmingly inflated estimates of the coal production that would be lost if it were passed. Not many really believed these estimates, except President Ford, who dutifully refused to sign the bill and gave it a pocket veto.

Laws which attempt to control the ravages of strip mining may be successful, and then again they may not be. The men who operate coal mines seem to believe that laws are made for other people, not for the mine operators, and they have some justification for such a belief. The mine operator has been a powerful economic force, often the only one in his community, and often he has managed to pay absurdly low taxes or even no taxes at all on his properties and mining machinery. The mine operators have banded together in powerful lobbies to secure the kinds of laws they have wanted, and they have exerted considerable pressure on supervisory agencies to ensure ridiculously lax enforcement of laws to which they object.

For example, some states have laws which require strip mine operators to restore the land to its original condition after the coal has been removed. The operator must post a bond to guarantee his compliance with this requirement, but all too often the compliance bond has been so low that the operator merely considers it an additional tax on his operation, and he expects to forfeit his bond when he moves on to devastate another area.

COAL CAMPS

The new machines have proven a mixed blessing in the coal fields. Although they have substantially increased output per man hour, this has served to reduce mine labor requirements at a time when coal production has also been declining steadily. In 1920, for example, coal supplied almost two-thirds of all the energy consumed in the United States. By 1960, when oil and gas had largely replaced it as a fuel for railroads and home heating, it had dropped to only one-fifth. Employment in the mines has been dropping even more rapidly than production, thanks to the new machines, and this has created deep economic distress for coal mining families and communities.

The coal camps of the southern Appalachians are among the most depressed and depressing areas in the entire United States. This is an almost unknown world. Few visitors wander onto the narrow roads which wind and twist, like blacksnakes in convulsion, along the mountain valleys. Few tourists are attracted to the dreary monotony of the mining camps which are all alike and merge imperceptibly, one into the next, along the narrow valleys.

Each camp is dominated by its giant black tipple, which now stands gaunt and abandoned at the end of a rusty siding, staring at the world through great eyeless sockets where its windows have been broken out. The second largest building in the company towns is the commissary, where the company maintained its offices and the store where the miners had to buy most of their needs, often at inflated prices.

The houses of the mining camp are ugly and unattractive, whether they are set in the rigid geometrical patterns of the company town or the random scatter of private construction. They are dusted, inside as well as out, with the soot and grime of the mines and tipples. Almost as soon as they are built they begin to look tired and old, as their tarpaper roofs and unseasoned lumber start to sag. The front of the house is adorned by a shaky porch, and the back yard by a privy, which as often as not pollutes the well from which the family draws its water.

Two or three rusting "junkers" sit in the front yard; the owner cannibalizes them for parts to keep one car running, and shoves them into the nearest creek when they no longer have anything worth salvaging.

Life has broken the spirits of many of the people of the coal camps who have grown old and tired before their time. Even if they were trained for it, there is no alternative employment locally. Some go elsewhere in search of work, but those who stay, and they are many, have the haunted eyes of the trapped. They must depend upon the kindness of others and the benevolence of state and national governments for the very food they eat and the clothes they wear. In camp after camp, most of the people are almost completely dependent upon some form of public assistance.

COAL AND INDUSTRY

Unlike the mining areas of the northern Appalachians, the coal fields of West Virginia and Kentucky have generated almost no industry, for the mines are owned and operated by absentee interests, and most of the coal is shipped out to other areas. The principal exception is the industrial belt which stretches from Ashland, Kentucky, to Charleston, West Virginia, and thence eastward along the Kanawha River.

Charleston is the largest city of the chemical manufacturing district along the Kanawha valley, which is often known as "Chemical Valley." Local deposits of coal, natural gas, and salt provide the raw materials for synthesis of a variety of basic industrial chemicals such as chlorine, sulfuric acid, and alkalies. Other important products of the valley include antifreeze, synthetic rubber, textiles, sheet glass, and metal products.

The Huntington-Ashland industrial district straddles the three states of West Virginia, Kentucky, and Ohio at the point where the Big Sandy River flows into the Ohio. The river terraces here were selected as the site for major railroad yards in the 1870s. The railroad terminus became an important Ohio River shipping point for the coal fields to the south, and evolved into an industrial center because of the ease with which raw materials could be assembled here by rail, river, and highway. The leading industries of the area produce metals (iron, steel, nickel, and Monel metal), transportation equipment, glassware, chemicals, and apparel.

RECREATION IN APPALACHIA

Once again, as it seems to do with each new generation, the nation has discovered Appalachia and its problems. Agriculture must be rejected as a possible solution for the region's economic ills and any extensive development of industry appears unlikely, at very best. An economic evaluation of three mountain counties in southwestern North Carolina concluded that "the current rate of growth would have to be doubled to bring the level of development up to that of the State in 8 to 10 years. The area needs more jobs; improved health, education, water, sanitation, and housing facilities; improved roads; better local shopping facilities; and community organizations for developing and implementing economic growth plans."[5] Doesn't sound like it has very much to begin with.

Most of the programs which have been designed to help Appalachia have not been successful. All too often they have concentrated on brick and mortar, on building new roads and schools and hospitals, on things which will impress a visiting Congressman or newspaper reporter rather than on helping people. Those who have needed help the most have been the ones who have seldom gotten it. For example, the "growth pole" approach has been a popular strategy of development; the idea is that money invested in a central urban growth pole will trickle down and stimulate the development of the entire region around it. The growth pole approach certainly has put money in the towns; the merchants, the doctors, the lawyers, and the courthouse politicians have prospered from the inflow of Federal funds, but precious little Federal money has trickled

5. Jack Ben-Rubin, *An Economic Evaluation of the Southwestern North Carolina Rural Renewal Area*, ERS-387 (Washington, D.C.: U.S. Department of Agriculture, Economic Research Service, 1968), p. iii.

back up into the hollows, where life still seems as grim and wretched as it ever was.

Most recently it has been suggested that the development of recreational facilities might serve the dual function of providing the outdoor recreational activities desired by the growing urban population of nearby areas along the eastern seaboard, and of alleviating some of the region's chronic economic distress by providing jobs for its people. The idea is not new. The cool uplands of Appalachia have been a welcome summer refuge for well-to-do people from steaming cities along the coast for two centuries. As early as 1778 people were resorting to "take the waters" at White Sulphur Springs, West Virginia, and the magnificent Greenbrier Hotel, which was built there in 1854, was one of the nation's great Victorian spas; it served as the "summer White House" for presidents from Andrew Johnson to Woodrow Wilson. Wealthy lowland planters in the Carolinas and Georgia began resorting for the summer to Asheville, North Carolina, in 1824, and the mountains around Asheville have become dotted with the summer second homes of prosperous Southerners.

The Blue Ridge Mountains of Virginia and the Great Smoky Mountains of western North Carolina and eastern Tennessee have two of the nation's most heavily visited national parks, partly because these areas are so close to the great urban concentrations of the East. The entrances to the Smoky Mountains National Park—Gatlinburg on the west, with more than fifty hotels and motels, and Cherokee on the east, with an unforgettable array of activities for tourists—are a veritable museum of uncontrolled commercial development.

The most remarkable recreational developments in Appalachia are products of snowmaking machines, which can cover the ground with manmade "snow" any time the temperature drops below freezing. The mountains of western North Carolina alone boast no less than eight winter sports areas, and skiing has become a fashionable activity in certain Southern circles.

Although some parts of Appalachia do have a very real potential for recreational development, attempts to attract large

numbers of visitors into the region will face almost insur-
mountable obstacles. It is difficult to get into Appalachia, and
once there it is even more difficult to move around. The region
has a thoroughly inadequate network of primary highways, to
provide access to it, and secondary highways, to provide access
to places within it.

Although the through roads are gradually being improved,
there are so few of them that they are clogged with boat trailers, camping trailers, and tent trailers, as well as trucks and
automobiles, and traffic often moves at a snail's pace. Most of
the secondary roads are so narrow, winding, and tortuous that
speeds greater than 30–35 miles an hour are positively danger-
ous, and head-on collisions with cars passing blindly on a hill
or curve are a common cause of death. Some of the more
interesting and scenic sites within the region can be reached
only by difficult footpaths or trails.

The visitor who does manage to arrive in Appalachia finds
much that is unattractive and even repugnant. This region has
far more than its share of automobile graveyards, unscreened
refuse dumps, and heaps of empty beer cans rusting along the
highways. Garbage and raw sewage are poured into many rivers and streams, whose waters are festooned with long, gaudy
chains of nearly indestructible plastic bottles during the spring
flood. Most of the towns are small and flyblown, with ancient
buildings, cracked sidewalks, and groups of idlers who casually
flick shavings from cedar "whittlin' sticks" into the piles which
litter the ground at their feet. Many public buildings have
signs—obviously disregarded—which proclaim fines for spit-
ting tobacco.

With a few notable exceptions, hotel-motel accommodations in most of Appalachia range from barely passable to
dreadful. The food is even worse than the accommodations.
No matter how much they may appeal to the natives, few
visitors will be entranced by such viands as fried "harmony,"
sirloin "stakes," beans threatening to congeal in the fat in
which they were cooked, or "country fried steak" which turns
out to be a very flat hamburger slathered with a suspicious
brownish paste masquerading as gravy. Furthermore, al-

coholic beverages may not legally be sold in many parts of Appalachia. Quite patently, the fact that a county is wet does not guarantee that it *will* have good eating places, but the fact that it is dry is much more likely to guarantee that it *will not.*

Although Appalachia has some superb State Parks, roadside rests, picnic grounds, scenic overlooks, camping areas, trailer parks, bathing beaches, and tourist information and welcome centers, most of these are already overcrowded. The region needs more tourist-recreation complexes with a full range of accommodations, services, and facilities. In particular, there is a great need for more extensive development of facilities for water recreation. Many Appalachian lakes and rivers are far from ideal for recreational activities because they are set amidst rugged topography which makes access difficult, because they lack natural sandy beaches, and because they lack such facilities as boat docks and marinas. In addition, many of these water bodies are polluted to some degree by seepage from coal mines, by municipal and industrial wastes which have not been adequately treated, and by household refuse which has been dumped indiscriminately into streams.

FORESTRY

If Appalachia has so little apparent potential for the development of agriculture, industry, or tourism, what then is the future of the region? The most obvious answer would seem to be to channel it in the direction in which it is already moving; that is, toward forestry. For example, successive Forest Surveys in eastern Kentucky showed that the acreage of forest land increased from 5,640 thousand acres (76 percent of the total area) in 1949 to 5,906 thousand acres (80 percent) in 1963.

Much of this area, unfortunately, is not efficiently managed for the production of wood and wood products. In 1963 only about half of the forest area of eastern Kentucky consisted of stands of sawtimber size. The remaining half was divided almost equally into stands of poletimber size and stands consisting predominantly of saplings and seedlings.

The problem of controlling forest fires must be solved as a first step toward improved woodland management, because this is an area where large numbers of fires are deliberately set. Whitaker and Ackerman, in their book on *American Resources,* tell of the elderly woman on her deathbed in the Appalachian hills who was asked what she most wanted before she died. She first hesitated, then said that what she most wanted was to see the woods on fire once more. Perry County, Kentucky, may be an extreme case, but the district forester estimates that its woodlands are burned at a rate equivalent to burning every acre in the entire county once every 20 years.

The next step, if effective fire control can be established, will be to convince forest land owners of the desirability of improving their timber stands by weeding out cull trees, proper thinning, and release cutting so that the most desirable species, such as yellow poplar, can make rapid growth. But the thought patterns of generations are hard to change, and it is hard to convince a person that trees can be a useful crop if he and his forebears have always thought of them as weeds.

The U.S. Forest Service has played a leading role in demonstrating techniques of effective forest management. The Forest Service has also been alert to the multiple-use possibilities of forest lands, and within the National Forests of Appalachia it has constructed and maintained camp grounds, picnic sites, hunting and fishing facilities, boat launching sites, hiking and nature trails, overlooks, and lookout towers.

6 The Limestone Lowlands

In contrast to the rougher hill and mountain sections of the Border Hills, the pattern of land use is simpler in the Limestone Lowlands which include the Great Valley, the Bluegrass country, the Pennyroyal Plain, the Nashville basin, and the valleys of northern Alabama (Fig. 6). Much of the land in these areas is used for pasture or forage crops, and livestock farming is the predominant agricultural activity (Figs. 12 and 13). Some of the Limestone Lowlands have developed distinctive agricultural specialties (Fig. 4). The Pennyroyal Plain of south central Kentucky, for example, has prosperous beef and dairy farms on which Burley and dark tobacco are grown. Cotton was once a major crop in the limestone valleys of northern Alabama, but in recent years the area has switched to intensive poultry production. The Shenandoah Valley of northern Virginia, a section of the Great Valley, is renowned for its apple orchards and turkey farms.

THE BLUEGRASS COUNTRY

Perhaps the most famous of the Limestone Lowlands is the Bluegrass country of north central Kentucky. The Bluegrass horse farms, which form a park-like belt around the northern part of Lexington, provide one of the most beautiful rural

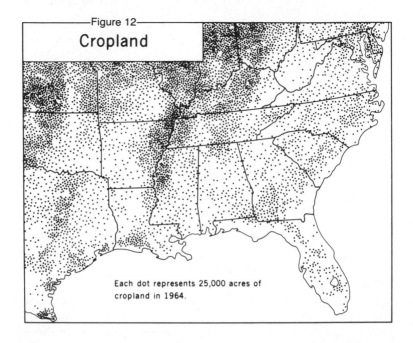

Figure 12

Cropland

Each dot represents 25,000 acres of cropland in 1964.

areas in the United States. Their lush green pastures, dotted with groves of stately trees, are enclosed by century-old slave-built stone walls and mile after mile of white board fence. On a horse farm of only 300 acres four men or more may be kept busy all year long doing nothing but painting the fences.

The horse farms are graced by elegant mansions and lavish horse barns. Many of the owners, wealthy men who also have fancy farms in other parts of the United States, visit their horse farms for only a few days during the racing season, and leave them in the care of a manager for the remainder of the year. The breeding, raising, and training of race horses can easily become a million-dollar operation, for a single horse may cost its owner as much as $75,000 before it starts its first race. The mares are bred to foal as soon as possible after the first of January, because that date is the official birthday of all race horses. In his first fall the yearling colt is put into training, and he usually starts to race in his second fall.

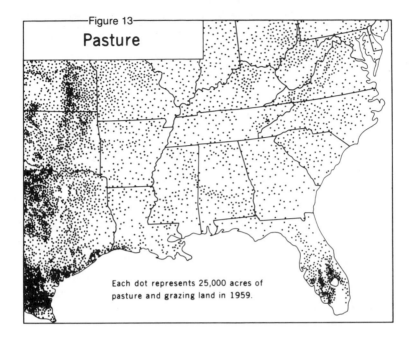

Figure 13

Pasture

Each dot represents 25,000 acres of pasture and grazing land in 1959.

In addition to its spectacular horse farms, the Bluegrass country also has many less pretentious livestock farms, with beef cattle and sheep and perhaps a few horses. Most of the farmers cut hay and grow a few acres of corn as feed for their livestock, but the most important crop of the Bluegrass is Burley tobacco, which is grown on almost every farm (Fig. 4). Even the showplace farms have 5 to 10 acres of tobacco, although their tobacco fields commonly are tucked away at the back end of the farm where they are less likely to be noticed.

Burley tobacco, which is a major constituent of cigarettes, differs in two important respects from the Bright tobacco that is grown in the Carolinas. The plant is harvested entire, instead of leaf by leaf, which necessitates a much larger tobacco barn. It is cured by hanging it in the barn to allow the leaves to dry, a process which requires a month or longer. The sides of the tobacco barns have vertical ventilators which can be closed in wet weather and opened in dry weather, to speed the curing process. If the barn is painted, the farmer often uses a contrasting color on the ventilators which gives the barn a distinctive striped appearance.

THE GREAT VALLEY

The Great Valley, another famous Limestone Lowland, is actually a series of connected limestone valleys which have served as a major routeway since the days before the Revolutionary War. Early German and Ulster Scot settlers landed at Philadelphia, moved inland until they met the barrier ridges of the Alleghenies, and then turned southwestward along the Valley. A whole string of towns and cities have grown up along the routeways followed by the early pioneers. These places served as commercial centers for the prosperous farmlands of the Valley and many of them have added manufacturing activities because of their excellent transportation facilities and abundant supplies of cheap labor. The manufacture of synthetic fibers, textiles, and apparel developed between the two world wars, and the manufacture of electrical equipment and metal goods has become increasingly important since 1945.

Roanoke, Virginia, started as a railroad town where the main line of the Norfolk and Western crossed the Valley on its way to the rich coal fields of southern West Virginia. Knoxville, Tennessee, is at the head of navigation on the Tennessee River and serves as headquarters for the Tennessee Valley Authority. Oak Ridge, the first city of the atomic age, is about 25 miles west of Knoxville. Chattanooga, Tennessee, is a diversified industrial center on the Tennessee River at the point where it turns westward and plunges into the hills of the Cumberland Plateau. This location was so strategic that two bloody battles were fought here during the Civil War, and it was from Chattanooga that General Sherman started his famous March to the Sea.

The southern end of the Great Valley has become the leading heavy industrial area in the South, and Birmingham has been nicknamed "Little Pittsburgh." Many of the ridges of the Allegheny Mountains contain deposits of low-grade iron ore which have been worked on a small scale at various times, but none of them has been so ideally located for the development of a major iron and steel industry as Birmingham. All of the necessary raw materials, including iron ore from Red Mountain to the south, and coking coal from the Warrior Basin of the Cumberland Plateau to the north, can be mined within 25 miles of the Birmingham mills.

Despite these advantages, the iron and steel industry did not develop at Birmingham until the Civil War, when an acute shortage of weapons forced the Confederate government to establish small iron works here for the manufacture of rifles and cannon balls. The industry grew rather slowly after the war, for local industrialists lacked adequate operating capital and the area was too far away from major national markets. Growth became more rapid after northern industrialists began to invest in the local concerns, but Birmingham has lagged far behind the other large metropolitan centers of the South (Table 3).

The principal blast furnaces in the Birmingham district are southwest of the city. They no longer depend on iron ore from Red Mountain, for much of the ore they use is imported from Venezuela through Mobile and up the canalized Warrior River. The iron and steel industry is also important in two other northern Alabama cities. Gadsden has steel mills, cotton textile mills, and rubber tire and tube factories. Anniston, a planned industrial center of the last century, has blast furnaces, textile mills, and large chemical plants.

THE TVA

Much of the southern Appalachian area is drained by the Tennessee River and its tributaries, which flow through parts of seven states and four physiographic provinces. The Tennessee rises in the Great Valley of southwestern Virginia and the Blue Ridge Mountains of North Carolina and Georgia, flows southwestward through the Great Valley in eastern Tennessee, cuts westward through the Cumberland Plateau into the limestone valleys of northern Alabama, and then turns northward in northeastern Mississippi to follow the western edge of the Interior Low Plateaus across Tennessee and Kentucky to the Ohio River.

In 1933 Congress created the Tennessee Valley Authority to harness the waters of the Tennessee River and to develop the resources of its basin in a unified fashion. The TVA has been an object of controversy since its very inception, and both its advocates and its opponents have been immoderate in their statements upon occasion. Although the Authority has been neither as wicked as some of its more violent detractors have claimed, nor as perfect as some of its more ardent supporters have believed, their very emotionalism has unfortunately tended to obscure the three basic missions with which the TVA was charged: to develop navigation, to control floods, and to generate electric power.

In order to accomplish these objectives, the TVA has built a system of multipurpose dams on the main stream and its tributaries. Eight dams on the main stream are the principal water-power producers. They have turned the river into a chain of lakes which extend from one dam to the next like a giant set of stair steps. Each dam has locks which raise or lower boats and barges from one lake to the next. Seventeen dams have been constructed on tributary streams, mainly in the Blue Ridge Mountains, to serve as storage dams which can supply water when it is needed for navigation or power production, or hold it when floods threaten. The storage dams also generate small quantities of power.

Kentucky Dam, just south of the confluence of the Tennessee River with the Ohio, is used primarily for flood control on the lower Ohio and Mississippi rivers. The waters of the entire Tennessee River system can be "turned off" by closing the gates at Kentucky Dam when these two rivers are in spate, and later released after the flood crest has passed. The TVA modestly admits that it averted $574 million in flood damages during fiscal year 1972–73 alone; the Authority has never been unduly bashful about telling the world of its accomplishments.

By 1945 the new dams and locks had created a channel 9 feet deep extending 650 miles upstream to Knoxville. River traffic has increased enormously since that date. Twelve general commodity river terminals and more than 100 special commodity terminals handle more than 28 million tons of freight a year; more than three-quarters of this freight either originates outside the area or leaves it. The principal commodities, according to weight, are coal for TVA power plants, building materials, grain, petroleum products, iron and steel, forest products, and chemicals.

Although TVA dams have a rated generating capacity of more than 5 million kilowatts, the ever-increasing demand for electricity in the TVA area since World War II has forced the Authority to shift from water to coal-fired steam plants to generate the basic power load. More than three-quarters of TVA's power in 1972 came from steam plants rather than from the river, and the proportion will increase in the future, because nearly all of the region's hydroelectric potential has already been developed. The Authority plans to shift increasingly to nuclear energy as a power source, and the anticipated capacity of 41 million kilowatts in 1982 will be 44 percent nuclear, 43 percent coal, and only 13 percent from the Tennessee and its tributaries.

Dependence upon steam power rather than water power for the basic load might seem slightly incongruous, but it enables the TVA to produce electricity flexibly and efficiently. Firing up a steam plant takes time, but starting a hydro plant is almost as easy as turning on a faucet, and supplementary power from stored water can be turned onto the line instantaneously whenever it is needed to meet peak demands.

The combination of cheap water transportation, floodfree waterfront plant sites, and cheap electric power has touched off an industrial boom in the TVA area. Electric power had already attracted the aluminum industry here before the TVA was created, and the surplus Army nitrate plant at Muscle Shoals, a left-over from the First World War, was the nucleus for developing a chemical fertilizer industry. Atomic plants were located at Oak Ridge during the Second World War because they needed such huge amounts of electric power. Since that war more than a billion dollars has been invested in waterfront industrial plants along the Tennessee, including electrochemical and electrometallurgical establishments, paper mills, aluminum reduction plants, fertilizer factories, grain mills, shipbuilding yards, and cement plants.

The striking developments that have taken place in northern Alabama illustrate the kinds of industrial growth that have been occurring all along the river. The Tri-Cities industrial complex (Florence-Sheffield-Tuscumbia) near Muscle Shoals has booming electrometallurgical, electrochemical, steel, and rubber plants. Decatur has become a major shipbuilding center for river barges, and imports grain from the Middle West for distribution to livestock farmers over a large part of the South. Huntsville, once a cotton trading town which used to boast that it was the "Watercress Capital of the World," has become the nation's leading rocket research, development, and testing center.

Another new development, which has been even more dramatic in recent years than the growth of industry, has been the phenomenal expansion of recreational activities on the new artificial lakes which have been created in a region where no natural lakes existed. The first systematic survey of the recreational use of the TVA's 11,000 miles of lakeshore, which was made in 1947, found 600 summer cottages, 9,600 pleasure boats, 7 million recreational visitors, and a total investment of $13 million in recreational facilities. A quarter century later there were more than 10,000 summer cottages, 52,000 pleasure boats, 60 million visitors, and $400 million worth of recreational facilities, including some of the nation's finest lakeshore resort state parks.

In 1963 the TVA created a unique demonstration area for outdoor recreation and environmental education in the Land Between The Lakes area of western Kentucky and Tennessee. This area is a peninsula approximately 40 miles long and 8 miles wide between the reservoirs formed by TVA's Kentucky Dam on the Tennessee River and the Corps of Engineers' Barkley Dam on the Cumberland. Just above the dams the two lakes are connected by a canal, which provides a passage between them for pleasure craft and barge traffic.

The Land Between The Lakes was sparsely settled before it was made into a park. The topography is hilly, and the soils, which are acid and have low inherent fertility, are generally unsuited to cultivation. Most of the land is wooded, with an abundance of wildlife, including deer, wild turkey, and beaver. The creation of 300 miles of shoreline on the two lakes has provided a remarkable opportunity for developing a combination of land and water recreational facilities such as picnic and swimming areas, 28 campgrounds with more than 1,100 camp-sites for groups and individuals, nature trails, riding trails, trails for off-road recreational vehicles, and a host of other activity areas. No commercial establishments are permitted within The Land Between The Lakes, but hotel, motel, and resort developments have mushroomed in the surrounding areas.

The spectacular growth of recreational activity along the ten thousand miles of TVA shoreline, and the industrial boom which is transforming the TVA area, are but two aspects of a major national enterprise in the integrated development of natural resources which has pulled together many local, state, and Federal agencies and activities. The multiple-use dam and reservoir system has accomplished its purposes of flood control, navigation improvement, and power generation, and the Authority has also worked actively to develop agricultural, forest, fishery, and wildlife resources. The TVA area has become a mecca for visitors from all corners of the world, and each year two to three thousand engineers and technicians from more than a hundred different countries come to study TVA activities.

7 The Growth Coast

The area within 50 miles of the Gulf of Mexico, and all of Florida, has been the most rapidly growing part of the South since the end of World War II (Fig. 2). Many factors have contributed to the population boom on the Growth Coast: the development of specialized agriculture; the abundance of raw materials such as oil and gas, and the growth of manufacturing based on the use of these raw materials; the growing importance of recreation, resort, and retirement areas in an increasingly affluent nation; and most recently, the advent of the Age of Space.

FLORIDA CITRUS

The production of citrus crops in Florida, which annually adds between a quarter and a third of a billion dollars to the state's income, is one example of highly specialized agriculture. Although early settlers from the north believed that wild oranges were native to the state, the orange tree had actually been introduced by Spaniards, who planted groves near St. Augustine as early as 1759. Indians were given some of the fruit and scattered the seeds widely through the state.

The citrus industry began to grow after Florida was annexed in 1821. Most of the early groves were in the northeast, near waterways, for overland shipment of the fruit was virtually impossible until the arrival of the railroads in the late 1880s. The growers in the northeast were bothered by periodic frosts and finally they were completely wiped out by the severe winters of 1894–95 and 1898–99, which pushed citrus production southward into the central part of the state.

The principal citrus producing district of contemporary Florida is in the south central part of the state (Fig. 4). The first plantings were on the warm sandy ridges of the central lake district. The preferred location for a grove is on the sloping southern or southeastern side of a lake, because heat radiated from the water moderates the temperature of cold winter air masses moving in from the north and northwest. The land should slope gently so that cold air, which is heavier than warm, can drain off downhill. The soil is not particularly important, for fertilizer science has reached such a point that almost any sandy soil can support a profitable grove.

Nearly all of the land on the ridge which is suitable for citrus has already been planted, and much of it has come under increasingly heavy competitive pressure for urban development because of the rapid growth of Florida's population in recent years. Lakeshore properties are especially desired for residences, and in recent years many citrus groves on the ridges have been bulldozed to make way for new housing developments. The national demand for citrus products has continued to increase, however, and hundreds of thousands of acres of new groves have been planted on the poorly drained flatwoods area east of the central ridge, especially by large citrus-processing corporations.

Florida has approximately a million acres of bearing citrus groves, which produce about three-fifths of the national crop. Seventy-five percent of the trees grow oranges, 20 percent grapefruit, and 5 percent tangerines and other varieties. Most of the groves run to 50 acres or less, and many of the grove owners have placed their land under the management of specialist caretakers, because modern machinery requires at least a hundred acres if it is to be operated profitably. A sizeable proportion of the grove owners do not even live in the areas where their groves are located; one caretaking company with 300 members has 60 residing outside Florida in 21 different states plus the District of Columbia.

A number of packing companies, which were originally organized only to pack and sell, have been forced to create their own caretaking departments to ensure production of enough fruit of adequate quality. All machinery including tractors is controlled by radio from an elaborate central headquarters with an office building, radio tower and transmitter, and separate sheds for tractors, machinery, fertilizers, and insecticides. The grove owner is charged for each operation performed on his land, and receives a credit for the crop harvested from it. He may request to have all charges placed against sales, and needs have no contact whatsoever with the grove other than the annual dividend check he receives when the crop is sold. His wintertime "business" trip to Florida to check on his grove is tax deductible.

The fruit destined to be sold fresh is taken to the packing house to be washed, dried, polished, waxed, graded, sorted by size, crated, and shipped off to market by truck or rail. In recent years, however, about 80 percent of the orange crop and almost 50 percent of the grapefruit crop have been processed into canned juices, segments, and frozen concentrates. Annual production of frozen orange juice increased from only 226,000 gallons in 1945 to 116,000,000 gallons in 1961.

An entire new industry has been created to solve the vexatious problem of waste disposal, since over half the fruit consists of peel, pulp, and seed. Citrus pulp has proven to be an excellent bulk carbohydrate feed for both beef and dairy cattle, with a feed value roughly equivalent to sugar beet pulp. Citrus molasses can be used to make industrial alcohol, and it is also a good energy feed for cattle.

RANCH COUNTRY

The availability of citrus by-products for feed has helped to stimulate the phenomenal growth of the livestock industry in central and southern Florida, where the number of cattle increased from less than ½ million in 1940 to more than 1¼ million in 1954. Cattlemen have crossed English breeds with the humpbacked Brahman to produce hybrids better able to withstand the hot, humid climate. The growth of the industry has been helped enormously by the eradication of screw worms. Even though screw worms had made life miserable for cattle in the area, the technique that was used to eradicate them seems like a rather dirty trick. Male screw-worm flies were trapped, subjected to heavy doses of radiation to sterilize them, and then turned loose to breed like mad, but completely without issue.

Large herds of cattle now graze former scrubland which has been converted into productive, year-round pasture by fencing and draining it, clearing the trees and underbrush, liming and fertilizing the soil, and planting improved grasses. Many Florida cattle ranches operate on an almost Western scale, local stores sell cowboy hats and branding irons, and small towns even boast rodeos. Cowboys armed with pistols, shotguns, and two-way radios ride the range in pickup trucks and light airplanes to watch for cattle rustlers, who can herd unguarded cattle into trucks and disappear with them in a matter of minutes.

The country north and west of Ocala has become one of the nation's leading areas for breeding thoroughbred race horses.[1] The rolling topography, well-drained phosphatic limestone soil, and large live oak shade trees remind horsemen of the famous Bluegrass breeding district in Kentucky, but winters are much milder. Skilled personnel such as managers, trainers, and exercise boys, are attracted by the mild winters, which are also better suited to raising and training horses. Plenty of local workers are available as grooms and field hands. Ocala did not become a major breeding center, however, until locally bred horses won the Kentucky Derby in 1956 and 1962, but now specialized services and facilities such as tack shops, feed stores, blacksmiths, veterinarians, and a range of top stallions stand ready to serve 5,000 horses on more than 160

1. Alice Luthy Tym and James R. Anderson, "Thoroughbred Horse Farming in Florida," *Southeastern Geographer*, Vol. 7 (1967), pp. 50–61.

farms which cover 30,000 acres. The owners, for the most part, are men who can afford to write off an average loss of a quarter of a million dollars or so a year on their horse farms.

THE EVERGLADES

The Everglades district in southern Florida illustrates a second kind of highly specialized agriculture. This low-lying plain extends southward more than 100 miles from Lake Okeechobee to the tip of the peninsula, with a slope of only 2 or 3 inches to the mile. The lake, whose surface is only 15 to 20 feet above sea level, had no natural outlet but simply overflowed along much of its southern rim at high water. The plain to the south is covered mainly with coarse, tough sawgrass, which may attain a height of 8 feet. The decaying sawgrass has formed one of the world's largest areas of peat and muck soils.

The area just south of Lake Okeechobee has been reclaimed by digging drainage canals and constructing a dike around the end of the lake, whose waters can be whipped into 10-foot high waves by hurricane winds. Although the peat and muck soils can be highly productive, they must be managed very carefully. After it has been drained, the soil may be destroyed by fires, which burn until they are put out by heavy rains. Furthermore, the drained soil is subject to subsidence, at a rate of an inch a year or more. In 1951 the Soil Conservation Service estimated that 88 percent of the original soil mass would have been lost within 50 years, and that much of the land would have to be abandoned for agriculture.

Despite these problems, as well as problems created by the necessity of careful water control and special fertilization with trace elements, the Everglades district has become an important agricultural area. Farmers on mucklands near the lake grow at least 30 different winter vegetables of which celery, sweet corn, cabbage, escarole, and beans are most important.[2]

2. Sidney R. Jumper, "Changes in the Areal Distribution of Commercial Vegetable Production in Florida," *Southeastern Geographer*, Vol. 5 (1965), pp. 24–32.

Their fields are large, and any field may be used to produce as many as four successive crops in the course of a single year. Special labor camps have been built for the migrant workers who come to do the harvesting and other stoop labor.

The peat land farther from the lake is used to raise beef cattle or to grow sugar cane. The high water table and sod cover of carefully managed cattle pastures hold soil subsidence to a minimum, but cattle also give the lowest return per acre. Many farmers rotate a few years of pasture with a few years of sugar cane, which is harder on the soil but is also far more profitable; the hot humid summers encourage prolific plant growth, and the cooler and drier winters are suitable for harvest, but killing frosts are rare.

Growing sugar cane looks like tall corn without ears. It is planted by cuttings rather than by seeds, and continues to produce new crops for several years without replanting unless it is winter-killed. Sugar cane production in the Everglades expanded enormously, from only 31,000 acres in 1956 to 198,-000 acres in 1967, with the arrival of refugees from Cuba who brought their know-how with them.

Although the drainage of the Everglades has created new agricultural land, it has also raised some very important questions of public policy in resource management. The new farm lands have been created by construction of some 1,400 miles of dikes and canals which block the natural southward flow of the waters from Lake Okeechobee, and divert them toward the Atlantic Ocean and the Gulf of Mexico. In the southwestern corner of Florida, through which these waters once flowed, is the Everglades National Park, third largest in the United States, a vast subtropical wilderness slightly larger than the state of Delaware.

When it was dedicated in 1947 the Park, which includes most of the area south of the Tamiami Trail (US 41), contained an astonishing variety of birds, animals, fish, and reptiles. The man-made drought, however, has wiped out the rookeries where tens of thousands of wood ibis and egrets used to nest each year. Ponds have dried up as the water level has dropped, and alligators have died unless they have been rescued and carried to deeper water holes by park rangers. The Army Corps of Engineers has belatedly constructed a canal to bring water back to the area, but nature lovers and conservationists have wondered whether efforts to control floods and create new farm land should be permitted to destroy a National Park.

Another threat to the Park was posed in the late 1960s, when the Dade County (Miami) Port Authority acquired a 38-square-mile tract of virtually untouched land in the Great Cypress Swamp with the intention of turning it into a badly needed new airport for southern Florida. The developers said that the area was populated only by "deer, alligators, wild turkeys, poisonous snakes, clouds of mosquitoes, and a tribe of Indians who annually perform a rite known as the Green Corn Dance," and a new jetport would bring in far more income and tax dollars than a few tourists and bird watchers.[3] The conservationists, however, showed that the Great Cypress Swamp supplied two-fifths of the water for the Everglades National Park, and they were able to secure Federal action to prevent construction of the jetport.

SUGAR COUNTRY

High value specialty crops, such as winter vegetables, are produced in many areas scattered along the Growth Coast, which enjoys the advantages of level terrain and a subtropical climate with a long growing season, mild winters, and abundant rainfall. On the negative side, much of the land is low-lying, poorly drained, and has soils of low inherent fertility. The winters do have an occasional killing frost, but are seldom severe enough to kill insect pests. Most specialty crops are grown for a relatively small and highly speculative market, with complex marketing problems and a constant danger of over-production.

Small wonder, then, that the Growth Coast has only one sizable area of continuous farmland, the Coastal Prairies and

3. *New York Times*, November 30, 1968.

marshes of Louisiana and Texas (Fig. 6), where sugar cane and rice are the principal crops (Fig. 4). The French settlers of Louisiana understood the facts of life on river bottomlands; the highest and best drained parts of the bottomlands are the levees, or the banks right next to the river, and the land slopes gently down and away from the levees into poorly drained backswamps. The French settlers put their buildings and roads along the levees, and laid out their farms and plantations in long narrow strips at right angles to the river. The normal strip, or long lot, was at least eight times as long as its frontage on the river.

Sugar cane was first grown commercially in Louisiana in 1795. Sugar plantations prospered when the United States placed a protective tariff on sugar after the area was acquired by the Louisiana Purchase in 1803, and the wealth of the large Louisiana plantations before the Civil War was legendary.[4] Sugar cane is grown on the rich alluvial soils of levees along the Mississippi River, Bayou Lafourche, and smaller streams. Yields in southern Louisiana are relatively low, because the active growth period for the plant is only about 7 months, as compared with 12 to 24 in most other producing districts.

The crop is planted in early fall. Entire stalks are placed in the furrows because sugar cane is grown from cuttings rather than from seed. Three crops normally are harvested before the field has to be replanted. The plants are cut by machine in late fall, the leaves are burned off, and the stalks are hauled to a mill where they are crushed to extract the juice. The tall mill chimneys and towering derricks for handling great bundles of stalks are distinctive features of the sugar country. Near the mill are rows of almost identical shacks for the workers, and a bit farther away, beneath the shade of moss-draped live oak trees, sits the handsome mansion of the planter. Most of the people are Cajuns, descendants of the French-speaking

4. John B. Rehder, "Sugar Plantations in Louisiana: Origin, Dispersal, and Responsible Location Factors," in John C. Upchurch and David C. Weaver, Editors, *Geographic Perspectives in Southern Development,* Studies in the Social Sciences, Volume 11 (Carrollton, Georgia: West Georgia College, 1973), pp. 78–93.

settlers who were expelled from Nova Scotia, or Acadia, in 1755 and brought to Louisiana in British warships. The Cajuns of the countryside are looked down upon by the Creoles of New Orleans, whose ancestors were also French.

NEW ORLEANS

New Orleans was founded in 1718 on the levee inside a great bend of the lower Mississippi River by the Sieur de Bienville, who laid out a gridiron street pattern thirteen blocks long and six blocks deep with a central square facing the river. This area became known as the Vieux Carré, or French Quarter. In 1763 New Orleans was transferred from French to Spanish possession, and after disastrous fires in 1788 and 1794 most of the French Quarter was rebuilt in Spanish style, with pastel stucco houses enclosing lush tropical gardens in central courtyards, and balconies with wrought-iron railings overhanging narrow sidewalks.

New Orleans was already a prosperous and bustling city when it was acquired by the United States as part of the Louisiana Purchase in 1803. The rowdy, upstart Americans were not welcome in the genteel French Quarter, so they established their own town on the levee upstream, on the other side of Canal Street. The principal streets in the new town followed the "long lot" boundary lines of the old sugar plantations, and ran at right angles to the river. New Orleans is inside a bend, so its main avenues converged on a desolate backswamp which was not drained until the twentieth century. St. Charles Avenue was laid out more or less parallel to the river, and about halfway between it and the backswamp.

Wealthy whites built flamboyant white-columned mansions with wide verandahs along the broad avenues, which are lined with live oaks, crepe myrtle, azaleas, and other subtropical plants. This part of the city came to be known as the Garden District, because its yards and gardens are in front of the houses, rather than in interior courtyards, as in the French Quarter. The picturesque Garden District is one of the largest and best preserved antebellum residential areas in America. The houses of black people and the poorer whites were back of the great houses along the avenues. The only really segregated area in early New Orleans was along the edge of the undrained backswamp, where the poorest black people lived.

The wealth and prosperity of New Orleans have always been based upon the city's location at the mouth of the richest river valley in the world. The cotton trade has been important, to be sure, but New Orleans serves the entire midcontinent, not just the South. Wharves extend for miles along the riverfront, but many are too small to handle large new container-ships and barge-carrying vessels, and a modern port is under construction in the marshes east of the city. Some of the obsolescent old river wharves are scheduled for replacement by waterfront parks.

Partly because it is a seaport, New Orleans has never completely lost its exotic flavor, and tourism is the city's second most important source of income. Each year millions of tourists bring even more millions of dollars to New Orleans so that they can stroll the picturesque streets of the Vieux Carré, shop in the boutiques of Royal Street, sip café au lait at the French Market, sample the famous Creole cuisine of the fine restaurants, and get a taste of sin in the nightspots of Bourbon Street, home of Dixieland jazz. A touch of Texas has been added by the construction of the Superdome, which cost only $35 million more than the original estimate of $30 million.

New Orleans has always lived in a precarious balance with Nature, but the modern city seems to be flirting with disaster. The highest parts are no more than 15 feet above sea level, and the entire city is below the level of the Mississippi River, which is restrained by man-made dikes. Since 1960 residential areas have been exploding into the drained backswamps, some of which are actually below sea level. Thousands of homes could be destroyed if the dikes were breached by floodwaters from the melting snows and heavy spring rains of the north, or by high tides lashed by raging hurricane winds from the south. Incidentally, the exodus of white people to the suburbs, where blacks are not welcomed, is building up a central city racial imbalance which threatens to end the long history of good racial relations in New Orleans.

RICE ON THE COASTAL PRAIRIES

Rice is the principal crop of the Coastal Prairies of southwestern Louisiana and southeastern Texas (Figs. 4 and 6). Cajun farmers in Louisiana had grown rice for their own use, but the crop did not become commercially important until the 1880s, and production did not spread into Texas until the twentieth century. Before that time the lush grasslands of the Coastal Prairies had been used only for grazing cattle, because the heavy black clay soil required systematic drainage before it could be cultivated. This area was developed by grain farmers from the Middle West who used the machines with which they were familiar to grow rice on a grand scale.

The rice growers constructed extensive drainage works but they also had to irrigate the land, for rice plants must be covered with about 6 inches of fresh water during most of the growing season. The farmers dammed streams and diverted water to their fields through canals, or they obtained irrigation water from wells. They enclosed their fields with low dikes 1 to 2 feet high which were high enough to hold irrigation water but still so low that farm machinery could easily pass over them.

Rice production in the Coastal Prairies is mechanized to a remarkable degree. Airplanes are used to scatter the seed and fertilizer and to spread insecticides and weed-killers. The fields run to 100 acres or more and the crop is harvested with the same kinds of combines that are used in the wheat harvest. The grain is hauled to elevators along the railroads and thence shipped to large mills to be dried, cleaned, and polished. Rice production in the United States is subsidized fairly heavily by the Federal government, and half to two-thirds of the crop is exported, mainly to Asia. Does it make sense to pay American farmers to grow feed for the people of India, Indonesia, and South Vietnam?

Most rice farmers on the Coastal Prairies rotate rice and

cattle. They grow rice one or two years, and then put the land in pasture for two or four years. The pastures benefit from the residual effects of fertilizer applied to the rice in addition to an ample moisture supply, and so this area has the densest concentration of beef cattle in Texas. Some farmers specialize in rice production, and rent their pasture land to ranchers.

BLACK GOLD

Much of the prosperity of the Gulf Coast is based on rich deposits of petroleum, natural gas, sulfur, salt, and shell lime, of which oil and gas are by far the most important. Deposits of oil and gas are trapped in geological pockets, called "fields," which are buried deep beneath the surface. These fields were difficult to locate in the days before modern geophysical prospecting techniques had been invented, and even today new fields are still being discovered.

Small deposits of oil and gas were known in eastern Texas shortly after the Civil War, but the first commercial well was not drilled until 1894, after oil had been discovered in a well being drilled for water at Corsicana. The first real boom began after a large gusher was brought in at Spindletop (south of Beaumont) in January, 1901.

Wildcatters began drilling in all directions and eventually discovered scores of oil and gas fields beneath a strip of land about 75 miles wide stretching along the coast from the Rio Grande to the mouth of the Mississippi River. Most of these fields are associated with huge underground salt domes, some of which contain deposits of almost pure sulfur in their cap rock. The salt dome belt extends far out to sea beneath the waters of the Gulf of Mexico.

Another great belt of oil and gas deposits extends from northeastern Texas across northern Louisiana and southwestern Arkansas into the southwestern corner of Mississippi. The first well in the fabulous East Texas oil field, one of the largest in the world, was brought in during September, 1930, and within 10 years this field had more than 25,000 producing wells.

Natural gas, which is found in many oil wells, was considered something of a nuisance before the Second World War. Much of it was burned as waste at the well, and the remainder was used as fuel for factories or as an industrial raw material. In recent years, however, interstate pipelines have carried this relatively cheap and clean fuel to homes in every part of the nation, and the one-time nuisance has become a valuable product in its own right.

WEALTH BENEATH THE WATERS

One of the most spectacular developments along the Gulf Coast has been the extension of mining out into the shallow offshore waters, which have become a veritable forest of towers. The search for oil has gone farther and farther out to sea since the first offshore well was drilled in 1938. Today oil can be produced profitably more than a hundred miles from shore in water up to 600 feet deep.

The boom in offshore drilling has tested the skills of naval architects, and proven a boon to shipyards along the coast. A self-contained drilling rig, bristling with cranes and tentacles, can cost 10 million dollars or more. It has its own engine room, workshops, storerooms, a tall drilling derrick, and air-conditioned living quarters and recreational facilities for 40 to 60 men. A helicopter deck sticks out on one side like a giant's ash tray. The workers are evacuated by helicopter when hurricanes threaten, but the rig itself must be designed to withstand the full fury of hurricane winds and waves.

The earliest drilling rigs were fixed platforms from which the equipment was removed after the well had been drilled, but floating rigs have become more common in recent years. All manner of ingenious devices have been used to keep the drilling platform stable by raising it above the surface of the water so that storm waves can pass beneath. Some drilling platforms have giant legs which are lowered to the sea bottom and then used to jack the hull above the surface. Others are supported by submersible barges which sink to rest firmly on the bottom when their hulls are flooded. Some of the newest deepwater rigs rest on semi-submersible barges which are poised delicately to float 50 to 60 feet below the surface, where they are not affected by wave motion.

Offshore oil exploration is a billion-dollar business. The Department of the Interior leases the right to drill on offshore tracts for $500 to $600 an acre, plus a yearly rental and a royalty payment of one-sixth of all production. The operating costs of the drilling rig run into thousands of dollars a day, and it costs about half a million dollars or more to bring in the average offshore well. The lessee has 5 years in which to find oil or gas, but he is permitted to use a depletion allowance of 27½ percent of gross production for income tax purposes, and he may charge off from other earnings all drilling costs other than materials used in the well.

Sulfur is also taken from offshore wells. Giant boilers at the sulfur mines heat millions of gallons of sea water to a temperature of 300°F, and it is forced down 1,000 feet or more into the sulfur deposit. The hot water melts the sulfur, which is pumped to the surface and piped into tankers which will carry it to market. As on the oil rigs, the workers on the sulfur rigs put in a week of 12-hour days, and then are flown ashore by helicopter for a week off.

PETROCHEMICALS, PORTS, AND SHIPYARDS

Petroleum is king along the Gulf Coast. Crude oil, as it comes out of the ground, is a complex mixture of hydrocarbons (chemical compounds of hydrogen and carbon) which must be separated before they can be used. The individual hydrocarbons vaporize at different temperatures, and they can be boiled off one at a time under carefully controlled conditions of heat and pressure. The petroleum refinery makes the "first cut," and removes the gasoline, kerosene, and lubricating oils. The residues, which are waste at the refinery, are the basic raw materials for petrochemical plants. The organic chemical industry transforms these basic chemical feedstocks (olefins and cyclics) into monomers, which are the building blocks for plastic resins and synthetic rubbers (polymers). The

polymers are the raw materials for factories which make mold-
ings, extrusions, and coatings: everything from vinyl flooring
and plastic toys to squeeze bottles, synthetic fibers, fertilizers,
drugs, and insecticides.

Most of the port cities along the Gulf Coast from Corpus
Christi to New Orleans have major oil refineries and petrochemical plants, which also line the Mississippi River as far
upstream as Baton Rouge. Pipelines bring crude oil to the
refineries, and a maze of pipelines carries petroleum products
between the towers, chambers, and tanks of the refineries and
their associated petrochemical complexes. Many of the harbors are naturally shallow, but they have been vastly improved
by dredging and canal works to provide cheap waterway connections with the East Coast, foreign countries, and—by Mississippi river barges—the Middle West. Abundant supplies of
fuel from oil and gas, cheap water transportation, and such raw
materials as oil, gas, sulfur, salt, and shell lime have provided
a base for rapid industrial growth in such cities as Baton
Rouge, Lake Charles, Beaumont-Port Arthur, Galveston-
Texas City, Houston, and Corpus Christi.

Fishing and shipbuilding have also contributed to the economic boom along the Gulf Coast. The principal species of
fish are menhaden, which are processed for industrial oils and
animal feed, and shrimp. An interesting experiment in auto-
mated shipbuilding has been conducted in the Ingalls Yard at
Pascagoula, Mississippi, which is the state's largest employer,
with a payroll of more than 10,000 persons. Traditional shipyards build a shaped metal hull, launch it, and then outfit it
with all the necessary pipes, wires, controls, and other internal
equipment. The Ingalls Yard has attempted to apply auto-
mated assembly line techniques to shipbuilding, moving from
components to subassemblies to modules which are put
together into a ship that is nearly complete before it is
launched. The idea looks great on paper, but it has not worked
out too well in practice, and the yard has run well behind
schedule, with cost and quality headaches which have been
widely publicized.

HOUSTON

Houston, the largest city in the South, illustrates many of the characteristic developments of the booming cities along the Oil Coast. Houston is 57 miles from the open sea on Buffalo Bayou, which flows into Galveston Bay. In the early days the city was a shipping port for cattle from the Coastal Prairies, cotton from the Blackland Prairie, wheat from the Great Plains, and lumber from the woodlands of east Texas.

In 1914 the Houston Ship Channel was opened to provide a passage 150 feet wide and 25 feet deep for seagoing ships. Today this Channel has one of the great concentrations of American industry. It is lined with the tank farms and gleaming steel towers of oil refineries and chemical plants. The waste of one plant may be the raw material of another. The whole complex, which is laced together by 1,000 miles of pipelines through which chemical raw materials and products can be interchanged, is so tightly intertwined that it is sometimes called the Spaghetti Bowl.

The 30 oil refineries in the Spaghetti Bowl have a daily capacity of 2 million barrels of crude oil, or about a third of the national total. Almost 400 different products are produced by 90 chemical plants here, including three-quarters of the nation's petrochemicals and half of its synthetic rubber. In addition there are warehouses and grain elevators, steel mills and cement plants, meat-packing plants and paper mills, and shipbuilding and repair yards. The port of Houston ranks third in the nation in terms of total tonnage.

Houston is a raw young giant. It is the only major American city with absolutely no zoning laws, and the vast sprawling metropolis seems to have been laid out almost completely at random. Twelve freeways radiate from the old downtown area, and free-wheeling developers have leapfrogged outward along them. Large expanses of vacant land have been left between outlying clusters of high-rise office buildings, luxury hotels, shopping centers, and residential areas.

Wells have pumped so much water out of the ground that

sizable sections of Houston are subsiding at a rate of six inches or so a year, thereby aggravating an already awkward flood problem in a city on low-lying level land which is regularly pelted by heavy thundershowers. The air hangs heavy with the stench of chemicals, and summers are so muggily oppressive that air conditioning is virtually a necessity. Perhaps the best symbol of Houston is the flamboyant Astrodome, fully covered to keep out the rains, and air-conditioned against the muggy air.

The quarter-billion dollar Johnson Space Center began operations about 25 miles southeast of Houston in 1963. The mission of the Center is to design and develop systems for manned space flight, to choose and train astronauts, and to plan and conduct missions. Millions of American television viewers have seen the long rows of consoles in the mission control center where flights into space are monitored. The Space Center has attracted the research offices and production plants of numerous companies which have aerospace contracts, and it has been largely responsible for the development of Houston's newest industry, the manufacture of data processing equipment, electronic computers, printed circuitry, and all manner of other electromechanical marvels.

THE AGE OF SPACE

Houston is not the only part of the South which has felt the magic touch of the Space Age, for this part of the nation has five major NASA installations. In the Manned Spacecraft Center at Houston the manned capsules are developed and tested and the astronauts are trained. Rockets and boosters are designed, developed, manufactured, and tested at the Marshall Space Flight Center in Huntsville, Alabama. Rocket production customarily is turned over to a private contractor after several prototype models have been built at Huntsville.

Huge booster rockets for Saturn and other large launching vehicles are made in the Michoud Facilities 15 miles east of downtown New Orleans, where PT boats were built during the Second World War. The Michoud Facilities are owned by the government but operated by private contractors. From Michoud the boosters are carried by barge to the Test Facilities in southwestern Mississippi for static testing. The test site is surrounded by a 200-square-mile buffer zone to reduce complaints about noise. From the test site the rockets go by sea to the Kennedy Launch Operations Center at Cocoa Beach, Florida, for final assembly and launching.

The nation's space program, which spent nearly $8 billion in 1966 alone, created many new jobs in the South. Hordes of engineers and technicians were brought in to develop and manage the program, and thousands of construction workers were hired to build control centers, assembly buildings, launching pads, and other new structures. New barge locks, causeways, and harbor dredging projects were needed along the Intracoastal Waterway over which barges carried the heavy rocket hardware.

The growth of Huntsville and Cocoa Beach shows what happened at the new installations. Between 1950 and 1960 the population of Huntsville grew from 16,437 people to 72,365. Brevard County, Florida, site of Cocoa Beach, shot from 23,-653 people to 111,435, for the fastest rate of county growth in the entire nation. The list of firms which established branch plants near Cocoa Beach reads like a veritable Who's Who of the aerospace and electronics industries: Bendix, Boeing, Chrysler, Grumman, IBM, I. T. & T., Ling-Temco-Vought, Lockheed, North American Rockwell, Pan-American, TWA. Real estate values skyrocketed with the construction of new homes, stores, roads, schools, hospitals, motels, and all the other services needed by a growing population. The German engineers and technicians gave Huntsville an aura of sober Teutonic propriety, but Cocoa Beach developed a real gold rush atmosphere with gaudy saloons and honky-tonks.

The bloom began to leave the boom when Federal spending on the space program was cut back in the late 1960s, and towns like Cocoa Beach began to learn the perils of excessive dependence on a single industry. Thousands of highly paid engineers and technicians were laid off their jobs or transferred, homes were repossessed or put up for sale at sacrifice prices, corner filling stations were closed, office buildings and factories fell vacant, motels went bankrupt, and Cocoa Beach began to seem like a ghost town to those who had known it during the boom.

Perhaps the most important long-term effect of the Space Age on the South has been the injection of new ideas. At least two-thirds of the new engineers and technicians came from other parts of the country, and many of them were impatient with traditional Southern values, especially racial segregation. Although Huntsville was well ahead of most Southern cities in desegregation, Dr. Wernher von Braun, Director of the Space Center and an outspoken critic of segregation in Alabama, argued that progress had not been as rapid as it should have been. He warned that continuing resistance to integration had complicated his problems of recruiting good people, and that it could deal a damaging blow to the state's multimillion dollar space industry.

TOURISM AND RETIREMENT

The Age of Space has added yet another tourist attraction in Florida, where tourists are the principal source of income. An estimated million people a year visit the Kennedy Space Center at Cocoa Beach, and several hundred thousand cars were parked in the areas around it to watch the spectacular launching of the first moon shot. The number of tourists visiting Florida each year has risen from around 5 million in the early 1950s to 30 million in the mid-1970s. The state has 100,000 hotel rooms, another 100,000 motel rooms, and 16,-000 restaurants to take care of visitors, and all manner of activities which are designed to separate tourists from more than 2 billion dollars worth of their money each year.

A string of resorts extends almost continuously along the east coast of Florida for more than 350 miles, from Miami Beach to Jacksonville. These resorts are the southern end of the strip that runs along the Atlantic Coast from Maine to Miami. One of the few remaining gaps, in South Carolina, was filled in quite rapidly during the 1960s with the development of elegant resorts such as Hilton Head Island, and less expensive areas such as the "Grand Strand" north and south of Myrtle Beach.

The east coast of Florida attracts visitors primarily from New York, Philadelphia, Boston, and other large cities of the Northeast; many of the visitors are Jewish. The west coast south of Tampa Bay, which began to develop rapidly in the 1950s, appeals more to people from the Middle West, and it is a popular retirement area for people who are tired of battling ice and snow. The north coast west of Panama City, which is part of the resort area that extends westward along the Gulf Coast, draws most of its visitors from adjacent states in the South.

Many of the people who visit Florida decide that it is a pleasant place to retire. Life is easy in the warm sunny climate, and the costs of clothing and heating are lower. Less than one-fifth of the state's citizens aged 50 and over are natives; the rest have moved to Florida from other states. The most famous retirement center is St. Petersburg, where 31 percent of the people in 1970 were aged 65 and over (as compared with 10 percent in the entire United States), but the development of new towns designed especially for retirement living has become a booming industry in the entire southern part of the state.

Florida has many attractions for visitors. Some come to escape the rigors of the northern winter, and to loll on superb beaches while acquiring the status symbol of a winter suntan. Others enjoy fresh and salt water swimming, boating, and fishing on 30,000 lakes and along 8,462 miles of coastline, a length exceeded only by Alaska. Spectators can go to the races and watch horses or greyhounds, and they can see polo, jai alai, yacht regattas, football bowl games, and the spring training camps of big league baseball teams. The state is famous for lovely gardens, for giant springs where the crystal-clear water of underground streams issues from limestone caverns, and for Indian villages, alligator farms, marinelands, lion ranches, and other man-made marvels.

A major new tourist attraction was launched in central Florida when Walt Disney World opened its doors southwest of Orlando in October 1971. The site was selected because it is near major highways, a major airport, and a metropolitan center in an area which has a mild year-round climate. The Disney people wanted a large tract of land where other activities would not compete with their business, so they established five separate corporations, none with the name Disney in its title, to buy 27,500 acres of land, an area roughly two-thirds the size of the District of Columbia. They paid an average of $185 an acre; in recent years choice commercial locations in the area have changed hands for more than $300,000 an acre.

The Florida Legislature obligingly created a separate development district so that Disney World could have complete authority over its own building codes, sewers, pollution abatement, storm sewers, fire protection, and other public services. One lake was drained, deepened, and refilled; sand from the bottom was used to create nice, white, sandy beaches around this lake and around a second which was excavated from swampland. The Disney people planned on at least 10 million visitors a year, and they figured on extracting an average of $50 from each one. It was anticipated that visitors would spend a day and a half at the Magic Kingdom complex, and golf courses, tennis courts, marinas, and other facilities were designed to keep them around for another day and a half. Disney World has a 12,000-car parking lot from which visitors are whisked by monorail or steamboat to the entertainment areas, campgrounds, or resort hotels with Polynesian, Persian, Asiatic, Venetian, and other exotic motifs.

Critics have complained that Disney World is a place of fantasy, a place to escape and forget all the bad things in life, and that it seems based on an implicit confidence in the immortality and mentality of Mickey Mouse; the Disney people, as the saying goes, have cried all the way to the bank. The owners of other tourist attractions in central and southern Florida have also complained because they feel that Disney World has cut into their own profits.

MIAMI

The most spectacular resort development in the South, perhaps in the entire world, is the Florida Gold Coast which runs north from Miami Beach to Palm Beach. Miami Beach is on a long sandbar separated by Biscayne Bay from the city of Miami on the mainland. An oceanfront strip along Collins Avenue in Miami Beach is lined with flamboyant skyscraper hotels, each of which tries to outdo the others in the way of odd-shaped swimming pools, ornate lobbies, plush dining rooms, basement arcades of fancy shops, star-studded entertainment, and garishly bad taste.

The Port of Miami has become the world's leading point of embarkation for winter cruises since the new $5 million terminal was opened. Ten ships operating out of Miami carried half a million cruise passengers in the mid-1970s, up from 100,000 in the late 1960s. Miami has taken over much of New York's former winter cruise business, because people from the North can have more time in the sun at sea if they fly to and from Miami.

Miami is only 2½ hours by jet from New York. The Miami International Airport, one of the busiest in the nation, is served by 11 domestic and 20 foreign airlines. Excellent air connections have helped make Miami the nation's "Gateway to Latin America." Many Americans have a vague notion that South America is somewhere south and perhaps a bit west of Texas, but in fact the entire continent lies east of Miami, and Miami has better air connections with the major South American cities than any city in Latin America. Major American corporations, such as Alcoa, Coca-Cola, Dow Chemical, Esso, Gulf Oil, and many others, have established their headquarters for Latin American operations in Miami, and the city has become a major international banking center.

The influx of refugees from Cuba has had a tremendous impact on the city's eating habits, entertainment, and even business. Cheap Cuban labor and retired New Yorkers have been responsible for the development of Miami's half billion dollar garment industry, third largest in the nation after New York and Los Angeles. Most Miami garment firms are small. Many were started by former Seventh Avenue manufacturers who came to Florida for a vacation and decided to stay. Their products have a large market in the South and in Caribbean countries, but buyers from all over the country are happy to use fashion showings as an excuse for a winter visit to Miami.

8 The New South

The attitude of most white Southerners, when they contemplate the future of their region, has been compounded of hope and fear. Their hope has been for rapid industrial development, which they have seen as the panacea which will transform the South from a retarded rural area into a region of modern cities and factories. Their fear has been the necessity of accepting the practice of racial equality, whether or not they accept it in principle. And the hope and the fear are inevitably interrelated, for cities are centers of change, and the growth of cities will bring increased pressures for integration.

CITIES OF THE SOUTH

Although the South has experienced rapid industrial growth in recent years, most of the cities of this region are still primarily commercial, distributing, and administrative rather than manufacturing centers. Some cities have made the change from rural market centers to modern industrial centers, but others have not. Some cities are lively, busy, and bustling, but many are still stagnant, drowsy, and torpid.

Most typical of the South is the small town which has grown up around the county courthouse in a rural county too poor

by-pass the industrial city?

130

to support more than one single town, and perhaps not even one. The center of town is the ornate courthouse. Facing it are the threadbare facades of banks, stores, flyblown cafes, and perhaps a shabby hotel. Between the stores are dingy staircases leading to the timeworn offices of doctors, lawyers, realtors, and insurance agents on the floors above. The Chamber of Commerce may be able to rattle off a list of all the reasons why the town is the ideal place to locate a new industry, and it might even be able to point with pride to a new factory out at the edge of town, but chances are that the factory was attracted mainly by the reservoir of cheap unskilled labor that was available in the surrounding rural area.

The towns which have grown beyond this stage to become cities are those which have enjoyed some superior advantage, such as easy access to major raw materials (as along the Gulf Coast), or location at a major transportation node, with attendant advantages for commercial and administrative activities.

Some of the oldest and most historic cities of the South, for example, are seaports along the Atlantic coast, such as Wilmington, North Carolina, Charleston, South Carolina, Savannah, Georgia, and Jacksonville, Florida (Fig. 3). Both Charleston and Savannah have set examples for other cities in showing how fine old buildings can be restored and adapted to modern use. Charleston is one of the most charming cities in the United States. The older section, on the peninsula between the Cooper and Ashley rivers, remains the most favored residential district, and still has much of its eighteenth-century atmosphere. The narrow, crooked streets have many fine old homes. Many of the houses are set sidewise to the street, and face narrow walled gardens. Railed porches running the full length of the house overlook the garden. The country around Charleston is renowned for the beauty of some of the old plantation gardens, which have been carefully tended for more than a century. They are at their best from December to mid-April.

Although the harbors of the South Atlantic ports suffer the handicaps of shifting offshore sandbars and shallow, tortuous, channels which can be maintained only by regular dredging, they have been made into modern ports by construction of docks, warehouses, storage facilities, and other harbor improvements. Port development has led to rapid industrial growth. The principal port industries include pulp and paper manufacture, oil refining, and the manufacture of chemicals.

The Gulf Coast also has some old and historic seaport cities. New Orleans, at the mouth of the Mississippi, is the nation's second port in terms of value of goods, and sixth in cargo tonnage handled. The newer ports along the oil coast to the west rely on petroleum and its products as their major export commodities, but New Orleans and ports as far east as Pensacola still obtain much of their business from Mississippi river barges. These ports have recently built large new grain elevators to handle cargoes of wheat, corn, and soybeans from the Middle West. New Orleans also imports tropical products such as sugar, coffee, and bananas. Mobile has special facilities for importing the ores of iron and aluminum. Tampa, on Florida's west coast, has become a specialized port for the export of phosphate rock, a major ingredient of chemical fertilizers, which is mined from great open pits a few score miles inland.

A second group of old and historic transportation centers are located along the Fall Line, where the tough old rocks of the Piedmont become buried beneath the less-resistant strata of the Coastal Plain. Streams flowing southeastward toward the Atlantic Ocean have cut waterfalls or rapids in their channels where they leave the tough rocks and start digging into those which are more easily eroded. These rapids formed the head of navigation on each stream, and were a natural transshipment point. A string of cities has grown up along the Fall Line, running south and west from Richmond, Virginia, through Raleigh, North Carolina, Columbia, South Carolina, and Augusta, Macon, and Columbus in Georgia to Montgomery, Alabama.

After the water power of the falls and rapids had been harnessed for industrial purposes, the commercial centers along the Fall Line became minor industrial centers producing consumer goods, especially textiles. Four of the Fall Line cities

(Richmond, Raleigh, Columbia, and Montgomery) have also been made the capitals of their respective states.

REGIONAL CAPITALS

Another kind of capital city in the South is the regional capital, which is best exemplified by Atlanta in the southeast and Dallas in the southwest. Both cities stand at the apex of the regional hierarchy, and both have the full range of goods and services of modern metropolitan centers. Both dominate the commercial, financial, industrial, and cultural life of their regions. Both began as railroad centers for prosperous hinterlands, and both have become major highway foci. Both are major air traffic interchange points, where passengers collected by regional feeder lines can catch trunk line flights to regional capitals in other parts of the nation. Both are major wholesale and retail centers. Both are major centers for banking and insurance, and both are seen by men of money as good places to invest in new developments. Both are aggressively modern.

Both Atlanta and Dallas enjoyed office building booms in the 1960s, skyscrapers downtown and planned office parks out along the freeways. The principal banks, leading law firms, and major professional and business services remain downtown, and the new office space in the suburbs is used primarily by the branch offices of large national corporations and by the regional offices of government agencies. Both cities have profited greatly from current trends toward national decentralization and regional centralization in many businesses. A regional capital such as Atlanta or Dallas commonly benefits when a national company decides to move some of its administrative or distributional activities into the South, or when a company decides to consolidate several offices in the South at a single location.

To a lesser degree, the function of regional capital is also performed by Memphis on the Mississippi, one of the world's largest cotton markets, by New Orleans, and by Richmond. At a still lower level, the functions of lesser regional capital and state capital are combined in Jackson, Mississippi, Little Rock, Arkansas, and Austin, Texas.

GOVERNMENT MONEY

The administrative function is quite important in the South, because government provides about one-fifth of all nonfarm employment in the region, and government jobs generally pay better than other nonfarm jobs. Federal spending has had a major impact on the geography of economic well-being in the South, but the precise dimensions of that impact are virtually impossible to measure; for example, Federal funds appear to have played a major role in the economic growth of Virginia and Georgia, but the experience of Florida and North Carolina indicates that they are not a prerequisite for such growth.[1] Federal civilian employment in the South has been of declining importance in recent years, but state and local governments have taken up most of the slack in response to ever-increasing demands for such services as schools, fire and police protection, and highway construction. Almost half of all state and local government employees in the South are engaged in education.

The principal Federal employing agencies in the South are the Department of Defense, the Post Office, and the Veterans Administration. Thanks to a benign combination of climatic advantages and Congressional seniority, this region has an inordinate share of the nation's military bases, which are a major addition to the economy of the areas in which they are located. Texans, it is said, "believe in standing four-square for free enterprise and full utilization of the Federal teat, and the rest of the South is not far behind."

The impact of a military base is illustrated by Pulaski County, Missouri, where Fort Leonard Wood is situated. The military population of the county rose from only 22 persons in 1950 to 23,904 in 1960, and the total population shot from

1. Clyde E. Browning, "Uncle Sam in the South: Federal Outlays to Southern States," *Southeastern Geographer*, Vol. 11, No. 1 (April, 1971), pp. 62–69.

10,392 persons to 46,567, achieving the second highest inter-censal population growth rate of any county in the entire United States. The area has poor farm land and precious few nonfarm jobs, so rural people drive in from miles around to take civilian jobs at the post; a survey in 1966 found that three-quarters of all jobs in the county were related to activi-ties at Fort Leonard Wood, and the average commuting dis-tance was 27 miles.[2] Few local business and service establish-ments had been developed, because virtually all military personnel lived on the post and used its facilities, but soldiers had to leave it for recreation, and the motel business had boomed along U.S. 66.

In 1970 nearly one million soldiers, sailors, marines, and airmen (49 percent of the members of the Armed Forces within the United States) were stationed in the South, a region which had only 30 percent of the nation's people (Fig. 14). The Hampton Roads (Norfolk-Newport News-Portsmouth-Hamp-ton) area in Virginia had more than 108,000 military person-nel; the San Antonio area and Fort Bragg, North Carolina, had almost 50,000 each; Camp Lejeune, North Carolina, and Fort Hood, Texas, had more than 36,000 each; and Fort Benning, Georgia, Fort Leonard Wood, Missouri, Fort Knox, Kentucky, Fort Polk, Louisiana, and Jacksonville, Florida, each had more than 25,000. More than 400,000 service people were stationed in these ten major military areas. Perhaps part of the nation's unfavorable image of the South may be attributed to the fact that few people cherish particularly happy memories of the place where they underwent boot camp or basic training.

CITIES AND INDUSTRY

Although manufacturing is an activity of growing impor-tance in most Southern cities, the South has no large industrial centers comparable to those of the Northeast or Middle West.

2. O. Wendell Holmes, *The Impact of Public Spending in a Low-Income Rural Area: A Case Study of Fort Leonard Wood, Mo.*, Agricultural Eco-nomic Report No. 135 (Washington: U.S. Department of Agriculture, Economic Research Service, 1968).

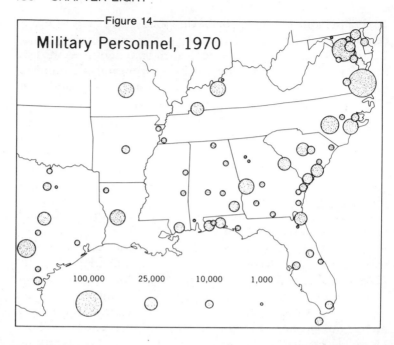

Figure 14

Military Personnel, 1970

100,000   25,000   10,000   1,000

Manufacturing in the South is predominantly for a local or regional rather than for a national market. The Southern city, by and large, is a place where the products of a trade area are processed and shipped, and a place from which the goods needed in the trade area are distributed. The industries which serve a national market are those which process local raw materials: the manufacture of textiles and apparel; of wood and wood products, pulp and paper, and furniture; of tobacco products; and of petrochemicals.

The South has a poor "industrial mix." The most rapidly growing industries, and those employing the largest numbers of workers, have relatively low value of product per worker, and low average earnings. One of the most widespread and rapidly growing industries in the South, for example, is the manufacture of all kinds of apparel. This industry is highly labor oriented, employs large numbers of women at low wages, and has been attracted to the South partly because companies can get away with paying lower wages than in other parts of the country. Many communities find consolation in the attitude that even a low-wage factory is better than no factory at all, and perhaps in time the workers will develop skills that might be useful in attracting new plants that will pay better.

Southerners like to boast about the rapid growth of capital investment in industry in the region, and they point with pride to new low-pollution factories that look for all the world like modern school buildings, and vice versa. The new plants depend on trucks rather than trains to transport their raw materials and finished products. Many of them are in rural areas, where land is cheaper and taxes are lower than in the cities.[3] Remote, scattered plants also make life tougher for union organizers. Twenty-five miles or more is no longer considered an excessive journey to work in a region where winter driving does not hold the same terrors as in more northerly climes. Long distance commuting to work in a factory has become a fact of life in the South, where the principal highway terrors are the car pools racing home at quitting time.[4]

The South needs new industries which will use modern techniques and machinery to produce goods of higher value per worker, and many states and cities in the region have been waging aggressive campaigns to attract such industries. A multitude of advantages have been cited for moving to the South. In an area which is essentially unindustrialized, the new employer can have the cream of the labor force, and at lower wage rates. Plant sites are cheap, winters are milder, and costs of living are lower. Power costs are favorable, water supplies are ample, and raw materials are abundant. The regional market is growing, and facilities for transportation and communication are improving. State and municipal taxes are lower, and

3. Richard E. Lonsdale and Clyde E. Browning, "Rural-Urban Locational Preferences of Southern Manufacturers," *Annals,* Association of American Geographers, Vol. 61 (1971), pp. 255–68.

4. Richard E. Lonsdale, "Two North Carolina Commuting Patterns," *Economic Geography,* Vol. 42 (1966), pp. 114–38.

some communities have even built new factories as an additional incentive.

Despite these advantages, the South has not been an industrial self-generating area in any major sense, for most of the region's industrial growth has resulted from the construction of new branch plants by large national corporations or by agencies of the federal government. Perhaps the best known example is NASA's creation of the Space Triangle, with the rocket research and development center at Huntsville, the spacecraft research and development center at Houston, and the final assembly and launching facilities at Cape Kennedy.

THE PLANT THAT FAILED

It is often argued that the development of industry will help to alleviate poverty in rural areas in the South. A survey of jobs in new and expanded plants in three poverty areas of the South in 1970 found that 26 percent were held by people who had been poor, and about two-thirds of these people had escaped poverty by their new jobs.[5] Three-quarters of the new jobs were held by people who had not changed their places of residence, the rest by natives who had returned to the area or by people who were attracted to it by the availability of work. Forty percent of the employees lived more than 10 miles from their jobs, and some commuted more than 40 miles each way.

The mere fact of establishing a factory is no guarantee that new jobs will be available to local people, nor is it any guarantee as to how long the new jobs will last. John C. Crecink has told the sad tale of the paper mill that failed in Pickens, Mississippi.[6] The mill seemed to have everything going for it. It was

5. John A. Kuehn, Lloyd D. Bender, Bernal L. Green, and Herbert Hoover, *Impact of Job Development on Poverty in Four Developing Areas, 1970,* Agricultural Economic Report No. 225 (Washington: U.S. Department of Agriculture, Economic Research Service, 1972).

6. John C. Crecink, *Rural Industrialization: Case Study of a Tissue Paper Mill in Pickens, Miss.,* Agricultural Economic Report No. 189 (Washington: U.S. Department of Agriculture, Economic Research Service, 1970).

in a former furniture factory which had closed down when the owner had died. Adequate initial capital was obtained from community, county, and state sources, both private and public, and a loan was made by the Federal Area Redevelopment Administration. The plant had excellent highway and railroad transportation, and all necessary utilities. A potentially adequate supply of pulp was available, and preliminary inquiries indicated that there was a market for the tissue which was to be manufactured. The plant was expected to provide 100 new jobs in an area which needed them desperately.

The payroll at the Pickens plant never rose above 60, and within five years the plant had gone broke. What happened? Company officials said that on-the-job training of unskilled local workers had not been as successful as they had expected it to be, and most of the skilled workers had to be brought in from other areas. They blamed their failure on variability in the quality of the wet pulp they purchased on the open market, and the fact that their secondhand machines kept breaking down. Perhaps a more important factor than anyone connected with the operation seems to have realized was the fact that "the mill was unable to compete effectively with the larger, more favorably located producers." Geography simply cannot be ignored in the successful location and operation of manufacturing facilities.

THE PIEDMONT TEXTILE BELT

A primary explanation for the lack of greater industrial growth in many parts of the South is the absence of a supporting industrial complex. Modern industrial activity is highly interrelated, and a new plant must be located in terms of the satellite industrial complex necessary to support it. Most parts of the South lack such complexes, but two notable exceptions are the areas where much of the region's industry is already concentrated, the petrochemical belt along the Gulf Coast and the textile and tobacco belt of the Carolina Piedmont (Figs. 3 and 15).

Although the Carolina Piedmont textile and tobacco manu-

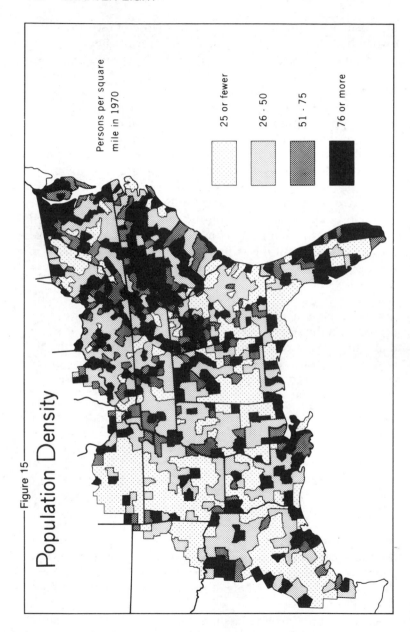

Figure 15

Population Density

Persons per square mile in 1970

25 or fewer

26 - 50

51 - 75

76 or more

facturing belt spills over into nearby areas, its core is an amazing string of cities extending southwestward from Lynchburg, Virginia, to Atlanta (Fig. 16). These cities are well served by an excellent network of railroads and highways. Most of them have grown at about the same rate, and no one city ever became truly dominant until Charlotte, North Carolina, began to emerge as a regional capital after World War II; Mecklenburg County, where Charlotte is located, shows as a hole in the map of manufacturing employment because of its diversified employment structure (Fig. 16).

The textile industry started to develop on the Carolina Piedmont after the Civil War when local communities pooled their capital and invested in new factories in a conscious effort to rebuild an economy shattered by war and by the fearfully low price of cotton.[7] The flat-roofed, red brick textile mills, three or four stories in height with high, narrow windows, looked for all the world like prison blocks. Their "inmates," white farmers who had abandoned their tobacco patches and fields of cotton and corn to work in the mills, were housed in drab mill villages, endless rows of monotonously look-alike cottages.

In addition to an abundant supply of cheap labor, the early Piedmont textile industry had plenty of cheap power, and the recently completed Southern Railroad was available to carry its products off to the industrial cities of the North. The streams flowing out of the mountains just to the west remain an important industrial attraction. The southern end of the Blue Ridge Mountains, where North Carolina meets Tennessee and Georgia, is one of the wettest areas in the United States, with an average rainfall of more than 50 inches a year. Not only is this water a source of power, but in recent years it has attracted a number of new factories, such as chemical

7. For an excellent essay on the development and distribution of manufacturing in the area around Charlotte, see Alfred W. Stuart, "Manufacturing," in James W. Clay and Douglas M. Orr, Jr., Editors, *Metrolina Atlas* (Chapel Hill: University of North Carolina Press, 1972), pp. 87–105.

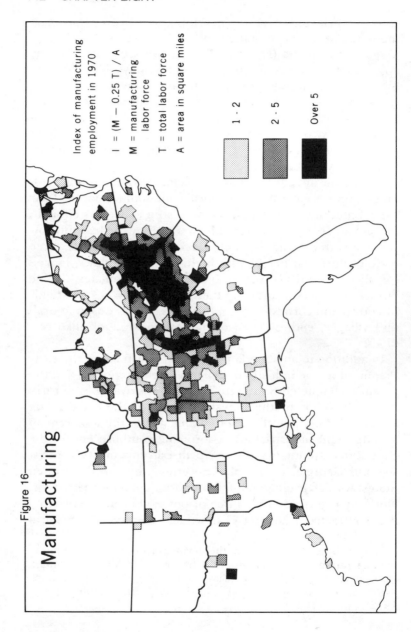

Figure 16

Manufacturing

Index of manufacturing employment in 1970

I = (M − 0.25 T) / A

M = manufacturing labor force

T = total labor force

A = area in square miles

1 - 2

2 - 5

Over 5

and paper plants, which require abundant and reliable supplies of pure water.

These new plants have brought a touch of industrial diversification to the Carolina Piedmont, although much so-called diversification consists of little more than developing manufacturing which has textile-related end-products: synthetic fibers, special machinery, apparel, and packaging. The Piedmont still is dominated by the traditional textile industry and, to a lesser degree, by the manufacture of tobacco products (especially cigarettes) and furniture. The tobacco industry is largely concentrated in Virginia and North Carolina. Richmond, Winston-Salem, and Durham are major centers, with vast warehouses for sales and storage, and large rehandling and redrying plants. The world's greatest concentration of wooden furniture manufacturing lies within a 200-mile radius of High Point, North Carolina. The furniture factories in this area produce almost 60 percent of the nation's wooden bedroom furniture and over half of its wooden dining-room furniture. Major furniture fairs are held four times each year in High Point.

ATLANTA

The area north and east of Birmingham is quite different from the rest of the South. Except for the Gulf Coast, the area west of a line running northward from Birmingham through Nashville, and south of a line running eastward from Birmingham to Charleston, has largely managed to escape the blessings of industrialization and urbanization. Most of the inland centers west and south of Birmingham serve as central places for retail and wholesale trade, and manufacturing is not a significant activity, no matter what their Chambers of Commerce may try to tell us (Fig. 16).[8] The area north and east of Birmingham has more cities (Fig. 3), more people per

8. John Fraser Hart, "Functions and Occupational Structures of Cities of the American South," *Annals,* Association of American Geographers, Vol. 45 (1955), pp. 269–86.

square mile (Fig. 15), greater employment in manufacturing (Fig. 16), and less poverty (Fig. 1), except for the hills of Appalachia (Fig. 17).

The main line of this urban-industrial South is the route of the Southern Railroad, U.S. 29, and Interstate 85, all of which run northeastward from Atlanta through Charlotte to Greensboro (Fig. 15). A parallel but lesser urban-industrial belt follows the Great Valley from Birmingham northeastward through Chattanooga and Knoxville to Roanoke. These two belts are separated by the Blue Ridge and Great Smoky mountains in Virginia and the Carolinas, but the mountains end in northeastern Georgia, leaving a fairly easy route between Chattanooga and Atlanta (Fig. 5). Atlanta, at the end of one belt and with easy access to the other, had become a major railroad center by the time of the Civil War, when it was devastated by a Yankee general named Sherman. The city was quickly rebuilt, and became the wholesale center and regional capital of the Southeast.

Atlanta straddles a low ridge between the headwaters of the Altamaha River, which flows to the Atlantic Ocean, and the Chattahoochee, which flows into the Gulf of Mexico. The historic heart of the city is the financial district, where five streets come together at Five Points. The business district has grown northward along one of these streets, Peachtree, a name so admired in Atlanta that it has been given to no less than sixteen other streets, avenues, lanes, places, circles, and drives, to the everlasting confusion of strangers. (Atlanta may also have the only street in the world named after Coca-Cola, a soft drink first concocted here in 1886, which has brought considerable wealth into the city.)

The ostentatious new skyscrapers of Peachtree Street give way northward to elegant residential areas which bloom with thousands of dogwood trees and azaleas in the spring. Far less attractive are the old ghetto areas down the eastern flank of the ridge, which were once the worst slums on the North American continent. Just east of Peachtree Street, in the Ebenezer Baptist Churchyard, is a simple stone reading "Free at last, free at last, thank God Almighty, I'm free at last," which

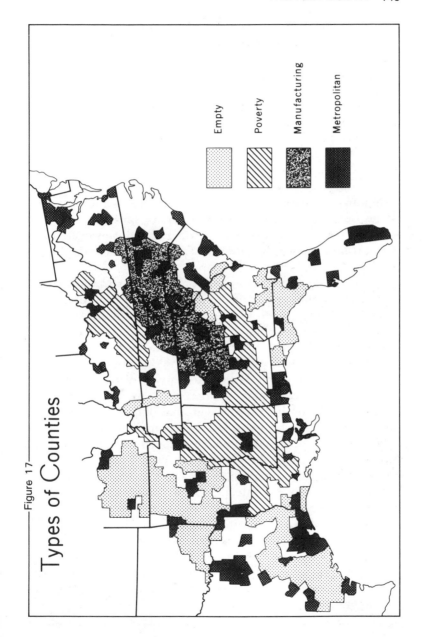

Figure 17

Types of Counties

Empty

Poverty

Manufacturing

Metropolitan

marks the grave of Martin Luther King, Jr., one of the leaders in the struggle for civil rights.

INTEGRATION AND POLITICS

Although racial integration is the most perplexing problem of the contemporary South, attempting to discuss it is rather like attempting to describe a boiling pot. Since February, 1960, when four Negro students touched off a massive onslaught on racial segregation by staging a sit-in at a lunch counter in Greensboro, North Carolina, the situation has been changing so rapidly that even the daily newspaper is sometimes out of date before its ink is dry. Despite the futility of trying to predict what lies in the days ahead, however, some background knowledge can provide a better understanding of changing events.

For example, one must begin with the fact that by any standard of social measurement, most Negroes in the South have been inferior to most whites. They have not been as well educated as whites. For the most part, they have had to hold menial jobs, have had lower incomes and lower standards of living, their lives have not been so rigidly bound by traditional Protestant morality; all of this has shown in many other less tangible ways. Any white Southerner worth his salt can cite case after case in which some Negro has defaulted on the most minor responsibility, or failed to accomplish a simple task.

Few white people in the South have become well acquainted with the better educated Negro teachers and ministers, whose duties bring them only into the most casual contact with whites. The average white person is completely unaware of their existence. In fact, Southern whites have remarkably little real contact of any kind with Negroes, and although the two races live together, they live almost completely separate lives. Those Negroes who have had regular contacts with whites have maintained good relations only by practicing the most abject subservience. It is a truism that nobody's cook believes in integration.

As a consequence, many white Southerners are genuinely

and honestly baffled by assertions that Negroes are their equals, for they have the evidence of their own eyes and their own experience that this simply is not so. They could quite as readily believe that ice is hot, or fire is cold, or black is white. The Southerner "knows" that racial characteristics really do exist, but he does not stop to ask himself whether these racial traits are the product of two and a half centuries of slavery plus another century of subservience and inferior opportunity. Whites have denied Negroes the chance to obtain an education, for example, and then criticized them as inferiors because they lacked it.

This, indeed, is the tragic dilemma of the modern South. Southerners and their forebears have created an inferior race, but now the nation expects the white people of the South to treat the members of this race as equal human beings. And this has given many white Southerners a desperate feeling of being trapped. No matter how deeply one may deplore it, one cannot dismiss the "Southern white syndrome" as cynical or calculated. No matter how wrong it is, it is deeply felt and deadly serious. No matter how irrational it is, it is a powerful emotional instinct.

The white leaders of the South have been unable to make up their minds how to resolve the tragic dilemma of their region. While they have vacillated and temporized, the role of leadership often was snatched by the less responsible members of society, the hate-mongers, the psychotics, the wild-eyed fanatics. The rest of the nation looked on in despair as these bigots revived a dormant regional tradition of physical violence and brutishness, of hard drinking and impulsive action, of cross-burning, lynching, and cold-blooded murder.

In the face of perceived danger, they forced the people of the South to close their ranks, like a besieged minority, and muffled all discussion. Every man was forced to take his public stand on the side of segregation, and the dissenter learned to hold his peace, or was forced to do so, or left the region. A few courageous whites, especially newspapermen, spoke out for sanity, but the majority drifted with the tide of passion. Those who stood against the tide, however timidly, became the targets of campaigns of intimidation. For example, Frederick Barger of Natchez was one of the three members of the Mississippi delegation who refused to walk out of the 1964 Democratic convention in Atlantic City over the integration issue. He returned home to discover that he had been branded a traitor by local newspapers. He received so many threatening letters and phone calls that he felt compelled to hire men to guard his home, and within the year he abandoned his lucrative law practice and left the state.

Changes in the attitudes of Southern leaders toward integration have come largely as the result of economic pressures. During the spring of 1965, for instance, businessmen in Vicksburg, Mississippi, largely ignored a series of civil rights bombings. Then the home of a branch plant personnel manager was bombed after he had started hiring Negro women for stenographic and clerical jobs, and the officers of the parent corporation became so aroused that they considered closing the plant. When civic leaders realized that they might lose the plant, they immediately launched a campaign against racial terrorism. Jackson, Mississippi, finally decided that the price of continued resistance to school integration was too high when a tractor manufacturer promised to move a 2,000-employee plant to the city if it would resolve its school dispute, and it did so immediately.

Although parts of the South moved slowly toward token integration, raw segregation still rode rampant in some parts of the region, where Negroes lived under a savage reign of terror, violence, and intimidation that would have made a Nazi storm trooper blush with shame. Negroes were afraid to attend public meetings or to cooperate with civil rights workers. They were dragged from their homes and flogged by night riders. Their homes were dynamited with crude homemade bombs. Negroes and civil rights workers were murdered, and the nation has been shocked more than once when juries have acquitted accused murderers. Local newspapers have paid scant attention to these trials, but have pounced with pathetic glee on reports of racial disorders in other parts of the nation.

Vigorous enforcement of school integration did not begin

until the Civil Rights Act of 1964 finally gave the Federal Government a financial club with which to ensure compliance with the Supreme Court decision of ten years earlier.[9] School integration, when it finally began, moved much more rapidly in the South than in the rest of the country. By 1972 only 25 percent of the black children in the South were in schools that were more than 90 percent black, as compared with 49 percent of the black children in the North and 53 percent in the Border states. The battle of school integration has moved from the rural South to the big cities, North and South, where whites have fled to the suburbs, leaving the inner city to the blacks. The new segregation is based on socioeconomic class, and the battle for racial equality is far from over.

Actual segregation still exists in many parts of the South where it has theoretically been abolished, for local authorities have complied with the letter of the law rather than with its spirit. Negroes in small towns and rural areas still know what is expected of them by the local white community. In theory they may sit where they wish in restaurants, theaters, and at athletic events, but the local Negro who insists on his rights soon discovers that segregation can be perpetrated by many subterfuges. He will be charged exorbitant prices, and receive inordinately slow service. He will probably be reported to his employer, dismissed from his job, and rated as a "poor credit risk" at the bank.

Integration will come most rapidly and effectively where contacts are most impersonal and economic reprisals are most difficult, in the larger cities, in restaurants and motels along the major highways, and in the chains. Civil rights activities have been facilitated by the anonymous nature of cities. Activities which might be fraught with danger in rural areas, where face-to-face knowledge and contacts are common, are less subject to retribution in urban areas. The city civil rights demonstrator may suffer physical violence, but not economic retribution; his life may be taken, but it cannot be ruined.

9. Mark Lowry, II, "Schools in Transition," *Annals,* Association of American Geographers, Vol. 63 (1973), pp. 167–80.

The increasing emancipation of Southern Negroes will have important political consequences. The Negro communities of the larger cities have spearheaded Negro participation in politics, and Negroes have been elected to public office from several metropolitan areas in the South. Increasing Negro registration will reduce the value of traditional racist demagoguery. In 1964, for example, returns from Negro precincts in Pine Bluff, Arkansas, showed a 98 percent vote for Johnson over Goldwater, but an 89 percent vote for Republican Winthrop Rockefeller for governor against segregationist Orval Faubus.

On the larger stage, Negro voters played a significant role in the 1964 presidential election, for it is generally agreed that Johnson carried four or five Southern states on the strength of the Negro vote, whereas the five states carried by Goldwater were those where the percentage of Negroes registered to vote was less than 45 percent.

The Goldwater Rebellion of 1964, which occurred almost exactly a century after the original War of the Rebellion, was a fascinating political and social phenomenon. Although Goldwater was soundly rejected by the rest of the nation, the white South took him into its bosom. The five states he carried were the selfsame five which had remained loyal to Stevenson against Eisenhower in 1952. Many of the counties which went for Goldwater in 1964 had never gone Republican in a presidential election since Reconstruction.

This dramatic shift reflects the growing split between the national Democratic party and its Southern wing. The average Southern white voted Democratic almost by instinct, and as late as 1956 the heart of the South remained Democratic when 57 percent of the total national vote went to Eisenhower and Nixon (Fig. 18). Short years ago it would have been unthinkable for a Southerner to cast his vote for any Republican, but he hates integration even more than he hates Republicans, and he has become more and more disenchanted with the national party's position on civil rights. Civil rights has been an issue of violent disagreement between the national party and its Southern wing at every Democratic national convention since the Second World War, and many Southern Democrats have

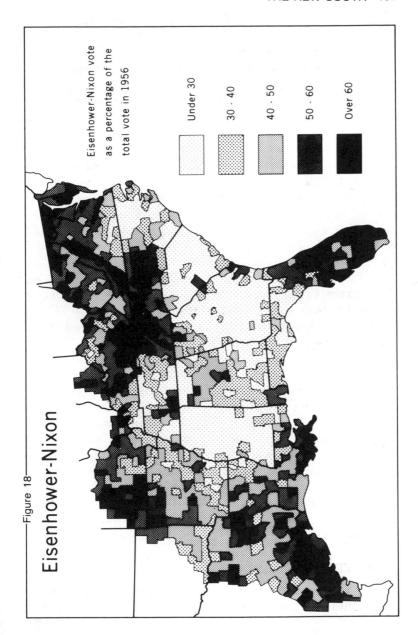

Figure 18

Eisenhower-Nixon

Eisenhower-Nixon vote
as a percentage of the
total vote in 1956

Under 30

30 - 40

40 - 50

50 - 60

Over 60

begun to feel that they have been told to accept the national party position or get out.

Their antipathy toward Republicans has been so strong, however, that they could not immediately bolt to the other party, and their initial mechanism for getting out was a variety of States Rights parties. In 1964 Goldwater received the legacy of the States Rights vote; few of the Southern counties which had once gone States Rights failed to give him their vote, and half of the Southern counties that voted for him had cast their vote for a States Rights candidate in at least one previous presidential election.

By 1972 the defection had become almost complete, and the change in voting patterns between 1956 and 1972 was startling (Figs. 18 and 19). The South appreciated Nixon's brand of racism, his opposition to busing for school desegregation, and his dedication to law and order. Senators from the South were his last bastion of support when he faced impeachment, and he knew the jig was up when even they finally realized that he did not belong in the White House.

Nixon's "Southern Strategy" apparently was abetted rather than handicapped by the candidacy of George C. Wallace, because the two seem to have appealed to different groups. Nixon attracted support from well-educated, middle-class, urban and suburban conservatives, who did not take to Wallace's brand of demagoguery and populism. Wallace did better in working-class areas, and he was especially popular with white voters in areas of high concentrations of blacks. At the risk of gross oversimplification, it is tempting to interpret contemporary Southern voting patterns in terms of three large blocs: the middle-class white party of Richard M. Nixon, the working-class white party of George C. Wallace, and the newly enfranchised blacks in the party of Lyndon B. Johnson. The names may change, but the principles remain the same.

THE FUTURE

And what of the future? Only the seventh son of a seventh son would dare attempt to predict what is going to happen in

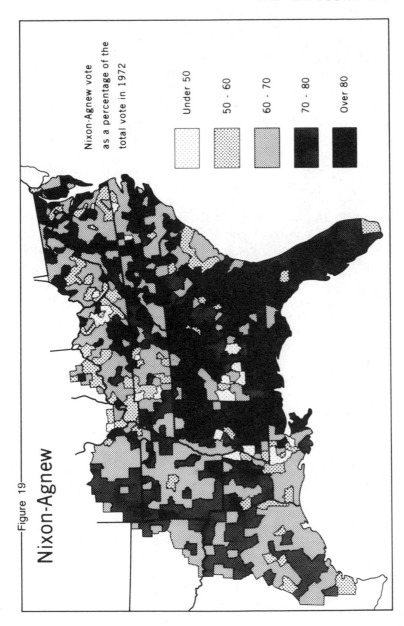

Figure 19

Nixon-Agnew

Nixon-Agnew vote
as a percentage of the
total vote in 1972

Under 50

50 - 60

60 - 70

70 - 80

Over 80

the South. The symbol of the South today, more than a century after Appomatox, is still the Confederate flag. After Reconstruction, as beaten Southerners began to rally and to regain their self-confidence, they adopted the proud banner of the Lost Cause as their symbol. This symbol of Southern defiance of the national will has served a multitude of uses, but never has it been so humiliated, defiled, and desecrated as it has by the wild-eyed fanatics who have wrapped themselves in it in their defiance of civil rights.

The Confederate flag is not only the symbol of Southern defiance, but it is a recognition of Southern inferiority, and the South is the nation's inferiority complex. The people of the South are fully aware of what the nation expects of them today, they are uncomfortably aware that they will be unable to live up to national expectations, and they are resentfully aware that the nation fully expects them to fail. No matter how carefully they may nurse their pride, and no matter how bold a face they may put forward, Southerners are completely aware that by national standards they are inferior, and have been inferior, for a century or more.

The people of the South have dedicated their resources to the wrong purposes. This region is torn asunder by the critical problems of learning how all its people may participate in the common decencies of contemporary American life. Southern defiance of the national will has absorbed some of the finest talents of its people in frustratingly unproductive efforts. The South has squandered one of its most valuable resources, the skill and ability of its people, in concentrating its efforts on its attempt to deny the Negro citizens of the region their right to the common decencies of American life. Despite its wealth of natural resources, despite its rich tradition, despite its fine and able people, the South can never realize its great natural potential and take its rightful place as a prosperous and healthy part of a great nation until all Southerners, white and Negro alike, endorse the principle of equal civil rights and decent expectations for all American citizens.

Suggestions for Further Reading

No one interested in the geography of the South can afford to ignore *The Southeastern Geographer,* the biannual journal of the Southeastern Division of the Association of American Geographers, which is published in the Department of Geography at the University of North Carolina in Chapel Hill, North Carolina 27514.

Arnow, Harriette Simpson. *Seedtime on the Cumberland.* New York: Macmillan, 1960.

Ayers, H. Brandt and Thomas H. Naylor. *You Can't Eat Magnolias.* New York: McGraw-Hill, 1972.

Bowman, Mary Jean and W. Warren Haynes. *Resources and People in East Kentucky: Problems and Potentials of a Lagging Economy.* Baltimore: The Johns Hopkins Press, 1963.

Braun, E. Lucy. *Deciduous Forests of Eastern North America.* Philadelphia: The Blakiston Company, 1950.

Campbell, John C. *The Southern Highlander and His Homeland.* Reprinted edition. Lexington: University Press of Kentucky, 1969.

Cash, Wilbur Joseph. *The Mind of the South.* New York: Alfred A. Knopf, 1941.

Caudill, Harry M. *Night Comes to the Cumberlands.* Boston: Little, Brown and Company, 1962.

Coleman, J. Winston, Jr., Editor. *Kentucky: A Pictorial History.* Lexington: University Press of Kentucky, 1971.

Daniels, Jonathan. *A Southerner Discovers the South.* New York: Macmillan, 1938.

Fogel, Robert W. and Stanley L. Engerman. *Time on the Cross.* Boston: Little, Brown and Company, 1974.

Ford, Robert N. *The Everglades Agricultural Area.* University of Chicago, Department of Geography Research Paper No. 42, 1956.

Ford, Thomas R., Editor. *The Southern Appalachian Region: A Survey*. Lexington: University of Kentucky Press, 1962.

Glassie, Henry. *Pattern in the Material Folk Culture of the Eastern United States*. Philadelphia: University of Pennsylvania Press, 1968.

Hansbrough, Thomas, Editor. *Southern Forests and Southern People*. Baton Rouge: Louisiana State University Press, 1963.

Hart, Freeman H. *The Valley of Virginia in the American Revolution, 1763–1789*. Chapel Hill: University of North Carolina Press, 1942.

Hart, John Fraser. *The Look of the Land*. Englewood Cliffs, N.J.: Prentice-Hall, Inc., 1975.

Heyl, James, Editor. *The South: A Vade Mecum*. Prepared for the 69th annual meeting of the Association of American Geographers in Atlanta, Georgia, 1973, by the Department of Geography at the University of Georgia in Athens.

Hoover, Calvin B. and B. U. Ratchford. *Economic Resources and Policies of the South*. New York: Macmillan, 1951.

Karan, P. P., Editor. *Kentucky: A Regional Geography*. Dubuque, Iowa: Kendall/Hunt Publishing Company, 1973.

Kniffen, Fred B. *Louisiana: Its Land and People*. Baton Rouge: Louisiana State University Press, 1968.

Lewis, Anthony and *The New York Times*. *Portrait of a Decade: The Second American Revolution*. New York: Random House, 1964.

McGill, Ralph. *The South and the Southerner*. Boston: Little, Brown, and Company, 1963.

Merrens, Harry Roy. *Colonial North Carolina in the Eighteenth Century*. Chapel Hill: University of North Carolina Press, 1964.

The National Atlas of the United States of America. Washington: Department of the Interior, Geological Survey, 1970.

Newton, Milton B., Jr. *Atlas of Louisiana*. Miscellaneous Publication 72–1. Baton Rouge: Louisiana State University School of Geoscience, 1972.

Parkins, Almon E. *The South: Its Economic-Geographic Development*. New York: John Wiley and Sons, 1938.

Raitz, Karl B., Editor. *A Tour of the Bluegrass Country*. Kentucky Study Series, No. 4. Lexington: University of Kentucky Department of Geography in cooperation with the Fayette County Geographical Society, 1971.

Robert, Joseph C. *The Story of Tobacco in America*. New York: Alfred A. Knopf, 1949.

Silver, James W. *Mississippi: The Closed Society*. New York: Harcourt Brace, 1964.

Surface Mining and Our Environment: A Special Report to the Nation. Washington: U.S. Department of the Interior, 1967.

Thornbury, William D. *Regional Geomorphology of the United States*. New York: John Wiley and Sons, 1965.

U. S. Bureau of the Census. *Census of Agriculture, 1969.* Volume V, Special Reports, Part 15, *Graphic Summary.* Washington: U.S. Department of Commerce, Bureau of the Census, 1973.

U.S. Bureau of the Census. *Census of Population, 1970. Number of Inhabitants, United States Summary.* Washington: U.S. Department of Commerce, Bureau of the Census, 1971.

Vance, Rupert B. *All These People: The Nation's Human Resources in the South.* Chapel Hill: University of North Carolina Press, 1945.

Vance, Rupert B. *The Human Geography of the South.* Chapel Hill: University of North Carolina Press, 1932.

Vance, Rupert B. and Nicholas J. Demerath, Editors. *The Urban South.* Chapel Hill: University of North Carolina Press, 1954.

Wigginton, Eliot, Editor. *The Foxfire Book: Hog Dressing, Log Cabin Building, Mountain Crafts and Foods, Planting by the Signs, Snake Lore, Hunting Tales, Faith Healing, Moonshining, and Other Affairs of Plain Living.* Garden City, N.Y.: Doubleday and Company, 1972.

Selected Topographic Maps

Professor Carl O. Sauer, in his Presidential Address to the Association of American Geographers in 1956, said "the first, let me say most primitive and persistent, trait of a geographer is liking maps and thinking by means of them. Show me a geographer who does not need them constantly and want them about him, and I shall have my doubts as to whether he has made the right choice of life. . . . We use them as actual guides and we enjoy them in armchair travel. . . . The geographer and the geographer-to-be are travelers, vicarious when they must be, actual when they may." The following list of topographic maps is dedicated to that instinctive craving of geographers. The maps have been listed alphabetically by states, and only the most striking feature of each map has been identified. I am deeply grateful to Merle Prunty for his help in compiling the list. The maps are published by the U.S. Geological Survey and are available in many libraries.

ALABAMA
Bessemer (1:24,000): iron and steel mills.
Cherokee (1:24,000): former cotton plantations.
Decatur (1:24,000): TVA river port with waterfront industries.
Farley (1:24,000): Redstone Arsenal
Goodman (1:24,000): peanut farms with air strips for crop dusters.
Mobile (1:24,000); major seaport with waterfront industries.

ARKANSAS
Barber (1:62,500): ridge and valley area of the Ouachita Uplands.
Evadale (1:62,500): drainage works on the Delta.
Smackover (1:24,000): oil field in the wooded sandy lands.
Sonora (1:24,000): orchards and poultry farms.
Whitmore (1:62,500): abandoned river channels and large cotton farms.

DELAWARE
Seaford West (1:24,000): poultry farms.

FLORIDA
Cape Kennedy (1:24,000): missile launching complex.
Cocoa Beach (1:24,000): aerospace boom area on offshore bar.
Havana South (1:24,000): shade tobacco farms.
Lake Harbor (1:24,000): sugar cane, vegetable, and cattle farms.
Lake Poinsett, Southwest (1:24,000): cattle ranches.
Lamont (1:24,000): woodland, marsh, and limestone sinks.
Naples South (1:24,000): resorts and mangrove swamps.
Ormond Beach (1:24,000): resorts on offshore bar.
Perry (1:24,000): forest industry land and paper mills.
Winter Garden (1:24,000): citrus production and processing.

GEORGIA
Cumming (1:24,000): poultry farms and circular city limits.
Darien (1:24,000): historic rice plantations.

KENTUCKY
Bardstown (1:24,000): distilleries.
Calvert City (1:24,000): TVA dam, chemical plants, and recreational
    facilities.
Horse Cave (1:24,000): tobacco sales warehouses at the foot of the
    Dripping Springs Escarpment.
Jenkins West (1:24,000): valley bottom coal camps.
Leatherwood (1:24,000): mining camp in isolated mountain area.
Lexington West (1:24,000): horse and tobacco farms, urban fringe.
Madisonville West (1:24,000): strip mines.
Paradise (1:24,000): strip mines and TVA power plant.

LOUISIANA
Crowley (1:62,500): rice farms.
Thibodaux (1:24,000): long lots and sugar plantations.
Venice (1:62,500): offshore oil field.
Westlake (1:24,000): oil refineries and petrochemical plants.

MISSISSIPPI
Midnight, Northwest (1:24,000): cotton plantation headquarters,
    cropper houses, gins, air strips for crop dusters.
Natchez (1:24,000): paper mill.

MISSOURI
Bonne Terre (1:62,500): Old Lead Belt.
Eldon (1:62,500): the edge of the Ozarks.

Kennett (1:62,500): drainage works on the Delta.
Viburnum East (1:24,000): New Lead Belt.

NORTH CAROLINA
Highlands (1:24,000): land abandonment and resort development.
Manchester (1:24,000): military base.
Norman (1:24,000): peach orchards.
Pantego (1:24,000): drainage of coastal swamps and marshes.
Rose Hill (1:62,500): rural cemeteries.
Rowan Mills (1:24,000): rural sprawl in the textile belt.

SOUTH CAROLINA
Dillon East (1:24,000): flue-cured tobacco farms and rural factories.
Greer (1:62,500): textile mills and circular city limits.
Hilton Head (1:24,000): seaside resorts.

TENNESSEE
Bethesda (1:24,000, photorevised): brush fallow.
Curtistown (1:24,000): Cumberland Plateau.
Daus (1:24,000): Sequatchie Valley, brush fallow.
Oak Hill (1:24,000): Knobs, suburban sprawl.

TEXAS
Kilgore, Northeast (1:24,000): East Texas oil field.
Pasadena (1:24,000): Houston Ship Channel "spaghetti bowl."
Port Aransas (1:24,000): offshore bar and tank farm.
Port Arthur South (1:24,000): oil refineries.
Schertz (1:24,000): military base.
Whites Bayou (1:24,000): rice farms and oil wells.

VIRGINIA
Abingdon (1:24,000): linear town in the ridge and valley area.
Annandale (1:24,000): suburban Washington.
Bent Mountain (1:24,000): Blue Ridge Mountains.
Charlottesville West (1:24,000): gentleman farms.
Norfolk North (1:24,000): seaport and naval base.
Norton (1:24,000): coal mines and coke ovens.
Winchester (1:24,000): apple orchards in the Great Valley.

WEST VIRGINIA
Belle (1:24,000): industrial Kanawha valley and strip mines in the
    Appalachian Plateau.
Blue Creek (1:24,000): oil and gas wells.
Charleston West (1:24,000): industrial Kanawha valley and sparsely
    populated Appalachian Plateau.
Racine (1:24,000): strip mines and oil wells in rugged area.

Index

Abandonment of land, 30, 43, 83–85
Acreage allotments, 36–37, 74
Aerospace, 124–126
Agricultural regions, 41–42
Agricultural specialty areas, map of, 26
Aiken, Charles S., 28, 36, 38, 41
Alabama, 6, 10, 13, 16, 17, 22, 27, 33, 40, 47–48, 54, 60, 63, 65, 88, 99, 102–103, 106
Alcoholic beverages, 20–21, 81–82, 97
Alluvial plain of the Mississippi River, see Delta
Anderson, James R., 63, 111
Appalachia, 78–107
Appalachian Land Type, 78
Apparel manufacturing, 136–138
Aristocratic tradition, 19
Arkansas, 6, 10, 13, 17, 25, 33, 39, 48, 52, 54, 59, 65, 78
Armed Forces, 134–135
Athens, Ga., 21–22
Atlanta, 14–15, 133, 141–146

Barns, tobacco, 71–77, 101–102
Bayou Lafourche, 115

Beef cattle, 39, 58, 61–65
Birmingham, Ala., 14–15, 102–103, 143
Black Belt, Alabama, 40, 44, 61, 63
Black people, see Negroes
Blackland Prairie, Texas, 10, 24, 39, 44, 63, 123
Bluegrass, Kentucky, 56, 99–102
Blue Ridge Mountains, 95, 103–104, 141
Boll weevil, 33–34, 59–61, 73
Border Hills, 78–98
Bourbon Street, 117
Breakfast cereals, 69
Bright tobacco, 72–75
Broilers, see Poultry
Brush fallow, 85–86
Buffalo Bayou, 123
Burley tobacco, 101–102

Cajuns, 17, 115–118
Capital, agricultural, 32–33, 41–42, 64, 66–67
Cash crops, 25–27
Cattle, 39, 61–65, 110, 113, 118–119; see also Beef, and tobacco, 75–77
Chattahoochee River, 22, 144

Chemical manufacturing, 121–124

Chesapeake Bay country, 70–72

Cigar wrapper tobacco, 75–77

Cities, 14–16, 130–146; see also Towns

map of major, 15

Citrus, 108–110

map of, 26

Civil War, 1–2, 73, 141, 154

Clearance of woodland, 39, 58–59, 85–86

Climate, 28–29, 114, 127

Coal mining, 89–93

Coastal Plain, 11, 25, 40, 132

Coastal Prairies, 11, 114–116, 118, 123

Controlled burning of woodland, 49

Corn whiskey, 81–82

Cotton Belt, 25–52

Cotton outside the South, 36–37

Cotton producing districts, 39–41

map of, 26

Counties, types of, map, 145

Cowboy regalia, 62, 111

Credit, agricultural, 32–33, 64, 66–67

Creoles, 116–118

Cropland, 10–11, 33

map of, 100

Cuban refugees, 113, 129

Dams, TVA, 104–106

Delmarva, 65

Delta, 10, 39, 43-44, 59, 79

Democrats, 22, 81, 150–154

Density, population, map of, 140

Depopulation, rural, 83

Depressed areas, 92–93

Disney World, 127–128

DLW (dried layer waste), 68–69

Eastern Shore, 65

Economic development, 2–5, 94

Education, 7–9

Effie's, 21–22

Eisenhower, Dwight D., 22, 150

vote for, map of, 151

Electric power, 104–106

Employment in manufacturing, map of, 142

Employment in mining, index of, 86–88

Employment in mining, map of, 87

Empty counties, map of, 145

Enterprise, Ala., 33–34

Everglades, 112–114

Facilities for marketing cattle, 64

Fall Line cities, 132

Fallow land, 85–86

Farming, 31–33, 82–83; see also Agriculture

Farm policy, 35–37

Farm woodlands, 46–48

Federal employment, 134–135

Feed companies and poultry, 67

Feed, livestock, 68–69

Fences, 63–64, 80, 100

Feuds, 80–81

Fire, forest, 47, 49–52, 98

Fires, forest, map of, 51

Fishing, 122

Flatwoods Land Type, 44–46

Florida, 11, 13, 17, 22, 27, 52, 57, 60, 73–77, 108–114, 126–129, 134

Florida parishes of Louisiana, 49–50

Flue-cured tobacco, 72–75

Forest, 46–58

Forest fallow, 30

Forest fires, 49–52, 98

map of, 51

Forest industry land, map of, 55

Forest land, 11, 47

Forest land, map of, 46

Forest, see also Woodland

Forestry, 97–98

Furnish for croppers, 33
Furniture manufacture, 143

Gadsden County, Fla., 75–77
Garden District, 116–117
Garment manufacturing, 129
Gentleman farms, 70, 100, 111–
    112
Georgia, 6, 10, 11, 21, 22, 27, 33,
    40, 52, 57, 60, 65, 67, 73–74,
    103, 134, 141, 144
Goldwater Rebellion, 150
Grand Prairie, Ark., 59
Grand Strand, 127
Grazing land, 11; see also Pas-
    tures
    map of, 101
Great Smoky Mountains, 95
Great Valley, 99, 102–103, 144
Groves of citrus, 109–110
Growth Coast, 108–129
Guano, 30

Hart, John Fraser, 10–11, 42, 71,
    85, 88, 143
Hay and pasture plants, 64
Heavy industry, 102–103
Hogs, 58, 61
Horses, 111–112
Horse farms, 100
Houses, 32, 116–117, 131
Houses, poultry, 66–67
Houston, Tex., 122–124
Huntsville, Ala., 40, 106, 124–
    126
Hydroelectricity, 104–105
Hypocrisy, 20–22

Idle land, 43
Illinois, 78, 88
Income, low, map of, 8
Income, median family, 5–6
Index of mining employment,
    86–88
Ingalls shipyard, 122
Integration, 146–154

Interior Low Plateaus, 104
Inner Coastal Plains, 40, 44
Iron ore, 17, 102–103
Irrigation, 29, 59, 118

Jews, 17, 127
Johnson, Lyndon B., 23, 150–
    152
Johnson Space Center, 124

Kanawha River valley, 93–94
Kentucky, 6, 10, 11, 13, 16, 78,
    80, 83–84, 89–93, 97–98,
    99–102, 104, 106–107
Kentucky Dam, 104–107
Kudzu, 64–65

Lakeshore recreation, 106–107
Land abandonment, 83–85
Land clearance, 85–86
Landforms, 24, 78–79
Landholdings, forest industry,
    54–56
Land Types, 43–46, 78–79
    map of, 45
Leasing of forest land, 56
Legislation, agricultural, 35–37
Limestone lowlands, 10–11, 99–
    107
Livestock, 39, 42, 58, 61–69,
    110–112; see also Cattle,
    Poultry
Livingston Parish, La., 50
Long lots, 115–116
Louisiana, 6, 10, 11, 16, 17, 22,
    33, 49, 52, 54, 114–119, 122

Management of citrus groves,
    109–110
Manned Spacecraft Center, 124
Manufacturing, 16, 135–143
Manufacturing counties, map of,
    145
Manufacturing employment,
    map of, 142

Manure, 68–69, 76
Marginal land, 84
Markets for cattle, 64
Marshall Space Flight Center, 124
Maryland, 13, 27, 65, 70
Maryland tobacco, 71–72
Matrons, bovine, 62
McCreary County, Ky., 82
Megalopolis, 23, 70
Memphis, 14–15, 39, 133
Metropolitan counties, map of, 145
Miami, 126–129
Midcontinent Land Type, 79
Migration, 11–14
Migration, Negro, 35
Military bases, 134–135
Military personnel, map of, 136
Mineral County, W. Va., 88
Mining, 86–93
Mississippi, 6, 9, 10, 13, 20–22, 33, 40, 50, 63–65, 104
Mississippi alluvial plain, see Delta
Missouri, 23, 78, 88
Monument to the boll weevil, 33–34
Moonshine whiskey, 67–68, 81–82

NASA, 124–126
Nashville basin, 99
"Nation's Number One Economic Problem," 2–5
Naval stores, 56–58
Negroes, 1, 6, 11–14, 19–20, 25, 117, 146–154
Negro migration, 35
New Orleans, 116–118, 132, 133
Nixon, Richard M., 22, 150, 152
  vote for, maps of, 151, 153
North Carolina, 10, 11, 13, 25, 27, 40, 57–60, 65–67, 72–75, 94, 95, 103, 134, 141, 144

Ocala, Fla., 111–112
Offshore drilling, 120–121
Oil and gas, 16; see also Petroleum
Oil refining, 121–124
Okeechobee, Lake, 112–114
Orlando, Fla., 127–128
Ozark Border Land Type, 79
Ozark Uplands, 23, 78, 83

Paper manufacture, 52–54
Part-owner farmer, 37–38
Part-time farming, 84
Pastures, 11, 61–62, 119
Pasture improvement, 111
Pasture land, map of, 101
Pasture quality, 86
Peanuts, 27, 59–61
  map of, 26
Peat soils, 58, 112
Pennyroyal Plain, 99
Perry County, Ky., 98
Personnel, military, map of, 136
Persons per square mile, map of, 140
Petrochemicals, 121–124, 139
Petroleum, 119–124
Pickens, Miss., 138–139
Piedmont, 25, 40, 44, 72–73, 132
Piedmont Textile Belt, 139–143
Plainsland South, 6, 10, 25, 33, 44, 58
Plant that failed, 138–139
Plantations, 27, 115
Plantation system, 31–33
Plantation tradition, 19, 61–62
Plantations, tobacco, 71
Politics, 150–154
Pollution, 96
Pollution from pulpmills, 54
Pollution from smelters, 88
Poor quarter of the nation, 5–7
Population, 11–14, 17
Population change, map of, 12
Population density, map of, 140

Population, farm, and tobacco, 75
Population growth, 135
Ports, 117, 122–124, 131–132
Poultry, 40, 65–69, 99
    map of, 26
Poultry houses, 66–67
Poverty, 4–9, 83, 92–93, 138
    map of, 8
Poverty counties, map of, 145
Presidential elections, 22–23
    maps of, 151, 153
Prestige of cattle, 61–62
Price of cotton, 35–37
Price supports, farm, 36–37, 74
Problem farm areas and poultry, 66
Productivity of the soil, 29–30
Prohibition, 20–21, 81–82
Protection, fire, 50–52
Prunty, Merle C., 31, 36, 38, 41, 62
Public administration, 134–135
Pulaski County, Mo., 134–135
Pulpwood, 52–54
Pulpwood mills, map of, 53

Quality of land, 43–46

Race horses, 100, 111–112
Racial relations, 4, 19–20, 126, 146–154
Ranch country, 110–112
Recreation, 13, 94–97, 106–107
Recycling poultry waste, 68–69
Regional capitals, 133–134
Regional identity, 17–23
Regions, agricultural, 41–42
Republicans, 22, 81, 150–154
Resorts, 13, 126–129
Retirement areas, 13, 126–129
Rice, 18, 25–27, 39, 59, 118–119, map of, 26
Rockets, 124–126
Rural depopulation, 83
Rural manufacturing, 137

St. Francois dome, 88
Sales warehouses, tobacco, 72
Salt domes, 119
San Antonio, Tex., 40, 135
Sandy Lands, 44–46
Sawmills, portable, 47–48
Scotch-Irish, 79
Second homes, 95
Segregation, 146–154
Self-deception, 20–22
Shade-grown tobacco, 75–77
Share-cropping, 31–33
Shawnee Hills, 78
Shenandoah Valley, 99
Shifting cultivation, 30, 85–86
Skip-row cotton, 38
Slaves, 1, 28, 31
Small towns, 14–16, 32
Soil, 29–30, 58, 76, 112, 114
Solid South, 22–23
Soul food, 18
South Carolina, 10, 11, 25, 27, 33, 40, 52, 73, 126–127, 144
South, defined, 23–24
Southern pine forest, 46–58
Soybeans, 25, 39, 42, 58–59
Space Triangle, 138
Spanish-Americans, 17
Specialty areas, agricultural, map of, 26
Spoil banks, strip mine, 90–91
Standard Metropolitan Statistical Areas (SMSAs), 15
    map of, 145
Starvation, 9
States Rights parties, 22, 152
Status symbols, cattle as, 61–62
Stills, 81–82
Strip mining, 90–91
Subsistence farming, 82–83
Sugarcane, 113–116
    map of, 26
Support price of cotton, 35–37
Swampland drainage, 58

Temperature, 28–29, 109
Tennessee, 10, 11, 13, 17, 22, 78, 88, 95, 103–107, 141, 144
Tennessee Valley Authority; see TVA
Texas, 10, 11, 13, 16, 17, 39–40, 52, 54, 63, 118–125
Textile manufacturing, 28, 102, 139–143
Thoroughbred horses, 100, 111–112
Tidewater plantations, 71
Tobacco, 3, 10, 25–27, 66, 70–77, 99–102
  map of, 26
Tobacco manufacturing, 143
Topography, 78–79
Tourism, 117, 126–129
Towns, 14–16, 32, 96, 102–103
Tree farming, 48
Triad of the South, 25
Turpentine, 57
TVA, 40, 102–107
Types of countries, map of, 145
Types of land, 43–46
  map of, 45

Ulster Scots, 79
Urban competition for land. 109
Urban places. 14–16
Urban rejuvenation, 131

Urban-industrial belt, 143–144
Urbanized areas, 14–16

Value systems, 17–23, 61–62
Vegetables, 70, 112–113
Vegetation, 46, 78, 85, 112–117
Vertical integration, 67
Virginia, 13, 16, 27, 59–60, 70, 72, 95, 99, 103, 134
Virginia tobacco, 72–75

Wallace, George C., 22, 152
Warehouses, sales, for tobacco, 72
Warrior Basin coal field, 89, 103
Water for livestock, 63–64
Water recreation, 106–107
Waterfront industry, 106
West Virginia, 13, 16, 78, 80, 83–84, 89–93, 95
Whiskey, 81–82
Wildfire, 49–52
Winter sports, 95
Winter vegetables, 112–113
Winter weather, 28–29
Woodland, 30, 46–58; see also Forest
  map of, 46
Woodland clearance, 58
Woods-burning culture, 50–52
Work ethic, 18–19
World cotton production, 36
Wrappers, cigar, tobacco for, 75–77

THE NEW SEARCHLIGHT SERIES

Akin, Wallace E. — THE NORTH CENTRAL UNITED STATES

*Alexander, Lewis M. — THE NORTHEASTERN UNITED STATES

Booth, Charles W. — THE NORTHWESTERN UNITED STATES

Bradford, Sax — SPAIN IN THE WORLD

Cutshall, Alden — THE PHILIPPINES: Nation of Islands

Durrenberger, Robert — CALIFORNIA: The Last Frontier

*East, W. Gordon — THE SOVIET UNION

Goodwin, Harold L. — SPACE: Frontier Unlimited

Hansen, Niles M. — FRANCE IN THE MODERN WORLD

*Hall, Robert B., Jr. — JAPAN: Industrial Power of Asia

*Harrison Church, R. J. — WEST AFRICA: Environment and Policies

*Hart, John Fraser — THE SOUTH

Hodgson, Robert D. and Elvyn A. Stoneman — THE CHANGING MAP OF AFRICA, Second Edition

Hsieh, Chiao-min — CHINA: Ageless Land and Countless People

Jackson, W. A. Douglas — THE RUSSO-CHINESE BORDER LANDS: Zones of Peaceful Contact or Potential Conflicts? Second Edition

Karan, P. P. and William M. Jenkins, Jr. — THE HIMALAYAN KINGDOMS: Bhutan, Sikkim, and Nepal

Kish, George — ITALY

Mellor, Roy E. H. — COMECON: Challenge to the West

Momsen, Richard P., Jr. — BRAZIL: A Giant Stirs

Morris, John — THE SOUTHWESTERN UNITED STATES

Mulvihill, Donald F. and Ruth C. Mulvihill — GEOGRAPHY, MARKETING, AND URBAN GROWTH

*Neale, Walter C. and John Adams — INDIA: Search for Unity, Democracy and Progress

Nicholson, Norman L. — CANADA IN THE AMERICAN COMMUNITY

Niddrie, David L. — SOUTH AFRICA: Nation or Nations?

*Nystrom, J. Warren and George W. Hoffman — THE COMMON MARKET

Patton, Donald J. — THE UNITED STATES AND WORLD RESOURCES

*Petrov, Victor P. — CHINA: Emerging World Power

Pounds, Norman J. G. — DIVIDED GERMANY AND BERLIN

Ramazani, Rouhollah K. — THE NORTHERN TIER: Afghanistan, Iran, and Turkey

Stewart, Harris B., Jr. — THE GLOBAL SEA

Wiens, Herold J. — PACIFIC ISLAND BASTIONS OF THE UNITED STATES

* These titles are available in a second edition as of 1976.